TO KARL AND MARK

This book m

1970

Philosophy of E

William K. Frankena

UNIVERSITY OF MICHIGAN

Sources in Philosophy

A MACMILLAN SERIES
Lewis White Beck, General Editor
THE MACMILLAN COMPANY, NEW YORK

Fifth Printing, 1968

Library of Congress catalog card number: 65–11067

THE MACMILLAN COMPANY, NEW YORK

COLLIER-MACMILLAN CANADA, LTD., TORONTO, ONTARIO

Printed in the United States of America

Contents

Introduction

I. PLACING THE PHILOSOPHY OF EDUCATION

Philosophy and education may be related in more than one way. One of these is indicated by the phrase "philosophy in education." Here philosophy is being thought of as one of the subjects to be studied or one of the abilities to be cultivated as a part of one's education. Another is pointed to by the phrase "philosophy for educators." Here again philosophy is being regarded as one of the things to be taught, this time to a special audience and possibly in a special form. In both of these ways of conceiving of the relation of philosophy to education, however, philosophy is being taken in its usual sense, and not as being about education. But, when we speak of the philosophy *of* education, we do not mean simply philosophy, we mean doing the kind of thinking that philosophers do, but doing it *about education*. The philosophy of education, properly conceived, does not just discuss philosophical problems in general, perhaps in the presence of educators and teachers; it discusses philosophical problems involving a particular topic, namely education.

What, then, is the place of the philosophy of education (a) in philosophy and (b) in the discipline of education? Let us consider its place in philosophy first. During much of this century the philosophy of education was represented as a part or offshoot of metaphysics and epistemology. Metaphysics is the branch of philosophy that deals with questions about reality—what things are real and how they are related to one another—and epistemology the branch that deals with questions about the nature and extent of our knowledge and about the definition and tests of meaning and truth. Thus it was thought that philosophers of education should be classified according to their theories of reality and knowledge. Now I do not deny that metaphysical and epistemological doctrines are relevant to questions about education. There certainly are points at which philosophers refer to or touch on their views about knowledge and reality in discussing education; for example, in the following selections, Whitehead does so when he talks about reverence in the last sentence of the first essay or when he says in the second that "each individual embodies an adventure of existence," and Maritain does so when he introduces "the philosophical-religious idea of man" in

1

opposition to the "scientific" one or criticizes the pragmatic theory of knowledge and truth. Dewey, of course, does so when he assumes that the scientific conception of man and the pragmatic theory of knowledge and truth, defended elsewhere in his works, are correct. In general, however, as the selections in this book show, the relevance of epistemological and metaphysical doctrines to the problems of educational philosophy is less considerable and less direct than it has usually been thought to be, and hence, it seems to me that the most fruitful way of thinking about the philosophy of education is to think of it as a part or offshoot of moral and social philosophy, as Plato, Aristotle, and even Dewey did. That is, it seems to me that questions about the aims, methods, kinds, program, and administration of education, are primarily questions of moral and social philosophy, and only secondarily related to epistemology and metaphysics. Metaphysical and epistemological doctrines may still be relevant in important ways, but, if they are, this will be only because they have a bearing on the problems of moral and social philosophy.

Coming now to (b), we must first notice that the term "education" may mean any of the following things:

(1) What parents, teachers, and schools do, or, in other words, the activity of educating the young,

(2) what goes on in the child, or the process of being educated,

(3) the result or what the child acquires or has in the end, namely, "an education," or

(4) the discipline of education, that is, the discipline that studies (1), (2), and (3).

Here, by the discipline of education I mean, then, not the *activity* or *process* of educating or being educated or the *result* of this activity or process, but the *field or subject* that studies and reflects on all of these and seeks to build up a body of knowledge and theory—descriptive, predictive, explanatory, or normative—about them, which may then be taught to teachers and school administrators or written out for them and for parents to read. In short, I mean roughly what is studied and taught in schools of education.

This discipline of education, like ancient Gaul and old-fashioned sermons, has three parts. *One* is the descriptive science of education, which seeks to discover and systematize the various kinds of facts, generalizations, and explanatory theories pertaining to the activity and process of education and to their result. In general, these facts, generalizations, and explanatory theories will be of the kind that belong to history or to such empirical sciences as psychology and sociology, for example, studies of learning or of objective testing; but, on some views, as on that of Jacques Maritain, they may be supplemented by certain nonempirical or nonscientific conceptions of man and the world drawn from metaphysics or theology. The *second* part is the normative theory of education, which consists of judgments or propositions about the ends or values at which the activity and process of education should aim, the principles they should respect or implement, the methods they should use, the curriculum to be followed, the kind of administration to be adopted, etc. These propositions may be relatively abstract, general, or theoretical—like Whitehead's statement that what education has to impart is an intimate sense for the power, beauty, and structure of ideas, together with a body of knowledge which has special relevance to the life of the individual; or relatively concrete, specific, and practical—like Dewey's call for manual activities in the schools. They may and presumably should be based on the kind of knowledge provided by history, psychology, and the science of education, in conjunction with normative premises taken from ethics and social philosophy, and possibly even with metaphysical and epistemological doctrines. Recent philosophers would add a *third* part: analysis. By this they mean, not the psychoanalysis of people, but the logical or philosophical analysis of concepts, statements, arguments, methods, and theories. Dewey is doing this when he defines education or analyzes the nature of thought, Peters when he discusses the role of aims in educational theory and practice, Maritain when he distinguishes knowledge-value and training-value. I am doing it here in this Introduction when I talk about the senses of education or the nature of the discipline and philosophy of education. Philosophical analysis of this sort is interesting in itself, but it is also helpful to both the descriptive science and the normative theory of education, since it aids them in being clear about their concepts and methods.

We can now place the philosophy of education. It does not belong to or include the descriptive science of education, though it may and should make use of this science. The philosophy of education consists, rather, of the other two parts of the discipline of education, that is, of the normative theory of education, especially in its more abstract, general, or theoretical aspects, and of the analytical philosophy of education. A philosopher who discusses education will then be doing either or both of these. If he does only normative theory of education, or both normative theory and analysis, but with emphasis on the former, then he is doing normative philosophy of education. Most of our authors are normative philosophers of education in this sense. If he devotes himself wholly or almost entirely to analytical thinking about education, then he is doing analytical philosophy of education. There is a growing emphasis on analysis among philosophers of education, just as there is among philosophers in general. Peters, who is somewhat less extreme than others, has been chosen here as our representative of this movement.

II. ANALYZING A PHILOSOPHY OF EDUCATION

There are many ways of introducing the philosophy of education, as just defined, to a student or reader. One is by writing out a systematic philosophy of education oneself, normative or analytical or both, as each of our authors has done. Another is by presenting and discussing the educational philosophies of a number of other philosophers, which is the method envisaged in this book, in accordance with the conception of the series to which it belongs. But, if we are to study and think about someone else's philosophy of education properly and profitably, particularly a normative philosophy of education, we must have a general scheme or model which will help us in analyzing, resynthesizing, and evaluating it, for the form and structure of a philosophy of education is not always made obvious by its author's mode of presentation. I shall now try to present such a scheme or model of a normative philosophy of education. In doing so I shall myself still be doing analytical philosophy of education.

We may distinguish between two kinds of abilities, dispositions, tendencies, states of mind, or traits of character or personality: (1) those which are innate, natural, or acquired so automatically that nothing properly called education is involved, for example, the ability to see or to think, or the tendency to breathe or to be affected by alcohol, and (2) those which are not, for example, the ability to skate or to think abstractly, the knowledge of geometry, or the trait of being just. The business of education is the acquisition of those of the second kind on the basis of those of the first kind. But of the second kind, some, like those mentioned, are or are taken to be desirable and some are not, and education is concerned only with those that are desirable. We do not ordinarily speak of the formation of bad habits as education. The activity or process of education is the passing on or acquisition of abilities, habits, states, or traits which are taken to be desirable by the agent involved (parent, teacher, or self), and which are not innate or automatically developed. Let us call these *excellences,* as Plato and Aristotle did. However, if the passing on and acquisition of such excellences were simply a matter of giving and taking pills, we probably would not regard it as education. Education is the transmission or acquisition of excellences (desirable abilities, habits, states, traits, etc.) by the use of techniques like instruction, training, studying, practice, guidance, discipline, etc.

There is room here for a good deal of philosophical analysis of such concepts as "ability," "habit," "trait," "knowledge," "thinking abstractly," "justice," "teaching," "training," "guidance," etc., but I must assume that they are familiar enough for us to go ahead. We may say, then, that the business of education is the promotion of certain excellences in the way of abilities, habits, knowledges, states, or traits. We may also say, as Whitehead does, that what education should aim at producing is men of a certain sort or certain sorts, but this only means men with certain excellences, and so comes to the same thing. Aristotle divided these excellences into intellectual ones and moral ones, and so it has been common to divide education into intellectual and moral education. Dewey and others, however, have insisted that some excellences are both intellectual and moral, namely flexibility, open-mindedness, integrity, straightforwardness, and acceptance of responsibility, thus breaking down this traditional distinction somewhat. And, of course, we must add physical excellences and physical education, and possibly still other kinds of excellence and education.

Consider now a normative philosophy of education such as is being offered by most, if not all, of our authors. It will ordinarily contain at least some bits of *analysis*—definitions, clarifications, distinctions, and the like—as we have already seen in examples from Dewey, Whitehead, and Maritain. Even more typically it will include some *empirical statements,* or factual claims whose truth or falsity can be determined by experiment or empirical observation. Examples are the following:

1. The formation of habits is a purely mechanical thing unless habits are also *tastes*. . . . (Dewey)

2. You cannot put life into any schedule of general education unless you succeed in exhibiting its relation to some essential characteristic of all intelligent or emotional perception. (Whitehead)
3. Not only does manual work further psychological equilibrium, but it also furthers ingenuity and accuracy of the mind, and is the prime basis of artistic activity. (Maritain)
4. The man who advocates authority and drill is most at home with things like Latin and arithmetic. . . . (Peters)

There may also be *metaphysical and epistemological doctrines* which are not so readily tested by the methods of experiment and observation; we have already mentioned some examples of these. Many writers hold that such doctrines are implicitly or explicitly present in every philosophy of education, but we cannot debate this here. In any case, however, a normative philosophy of education must contain statements and recommendations of a *normative* kind about the ends, principles, means, methods, subject matter, etc., of education, that is, statements about the ends that are *desirable* or *good,* the principles that *should* be followed, the means that *ought* to be used, and so on. It is easy to find examples in our selections:

1. All that we can be sure of educationally is that science should be taught so as to be an end in itself in the lives of students. . . . (Dewey)
2. The best education is to be found in gaining the utmost information from the simplest apparatus. (Whitehead)
3. The main function of the educator is to pass on this priceless human heritage [of rules, information and skills]. (Peters)
4. For the main point is surely to be a good man rather than to be a learned man. (Maritain)

It should be noted here that it is not always easy to tell if a given statement belongs to one of these four kinds or to another. Take, for example, the following:

1. In last analysis, *all* that the educator can do is modify stimuli so that response will as surely as is possible result in the formation of desirable intellectual and emotional dispositions. (Dewey)
2. Thinking *is* the method of intelligent learning, of learning that employs and rewards mind. (Dewey)
3. There is only one subject-matter for education, and that is Life in all its manifestations. (Whitehead)
4. But the only avenue towards knowledge is by discipline in the acquirement of ordered fact. (Whitehead)

5. . . . it is by grasping the object and having itself seized and vitalized by truth that the human mind gains both its strength and its freedom. (Maritain)

These sentences are ambiguous or perhaps ambivalent, though in different ways. For example, (1) may be factual or normative; (2) and (3) definitional or normative; (4) empirical or epistemological; (5) empirical, metaphysical, or normative. What is being said or done in a sentence is not always clear, but a reader must try to determine what it is from its context and from its apparent place in the philosophy of education being presented. It is important that he do this carefully, if he is to understand what is going on and why.

However, a normative philosophy of education is not a mere conjunction of sentences of these four kinds, though it may seem so when one reads some of our authors. To get such a philosophy of education clearly in mind one must fit these different kinds of statements into a certain pattern of organization, and I shall borrow from John Stuart Mill's *System of Logic,* Book VI, Chapters V and XII, with adaptations, in order to explain this. Mill points out that every practical art like education has as its *conclusions* a number of practical precepts about what should be done and how it should be done. But, if it is at all philosophical in character, it will also provide a line of *reasoning* to justify these practical conclusions. To do this it must tell us what excellences we are to produce in people, and then show us, by appeal to the facts of psychology, sociology, and the science of education, what means, etc., we are to use in producing them. This part of its reasoning may be represented thus:

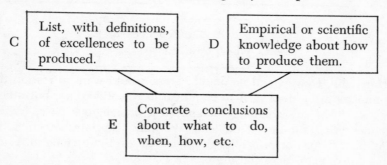

Mill adds, however, that a philosophy of education must also provide an adequate rationale, not only for the precepts included in E, but for the list of excellences given in C. This involves a second level of thinking, and it is here especially that philosophy comes in. To provide it one must put down what one takes to be the basic ends or principles of ethical and social philosophy (this is why the philosophy of education is an offshoot of ethics and social philosophy), and then show that these ends or principles require us to cultivate the abilities, traits, etc., listed in C—that is, that, if we are to promote these ends or act on these principles, then we must foster those abilities, traits, etc. In other words, to make a case for what one includes in C, one needs both basic ends or principles, *and* empirical or other beliefs or knowledge showing what abilities, traits, etc., are necessary for carrying out these ends or principles. Mill was a utilitarian, that is, he thought that the basic end was the greatest general happiness—or alternatively that the basic principle was the "principle of utility"—but different philosophers take different views about this and some of them are not utilitarians. Of course, they also differ about whether beliefs about basic ends or principles can be justified in their turn (and, if so, how), and some would say they must be grounded in metaphysical or theological premises; but this raises questions which belong to philosophy in general and not to the philosophy of education proper.

This higher level of reasoning may be schematized as follows:

A	Statement of basic ends or principles of ethics and social thought.	B	Empirical and other premises about human nature, life, and the world.

C	List of excellences to be produced.

Here Mill, Dewey, and no doubt Peters, would want to restrict the premises to be used in B to empirical or scientific ones, but others would insist on including metaphysical or religious ones, for instance, Maritain and Whitehead. We may also note here that the "ultimate" ends or principles of education are those given in A and the "proximate" ones those given in C.

A normative philosophy of education, therefore, has two parts, (1) a comparatively philosophical and theoretical line of reasoning, involving A, B, and C, to show what excellences are to be cultivated by education, and (2) a comparatively empirical or scientific and practical line of reasoning, involving C again and D and E, to show how and when they are to be cultivated. The conclusions of the first part become premises of the second part, as is shown by the following picture:

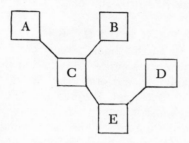

Mill talks as if the propositions in D are to be derived wholly or at least in part from those in B, and they may be, but they need not be. It may also be that some of the practical conclusions in E follow directly from the statement of basic ends or principles in A, together with statements from B or C. An example of this is the conclusion already quoted from Dewey to the effect that science should be taught so as to be an end in itself in the lives of the students, if this is understood as following from a previous conclusion that science is to be taught together with a basic principle to the effect that students must be respected and treated as persons in their own right. (It may, however, also be thought of as following from the previous conclusion that science is to be taught plus the factual premise that science is more effectively taught if introduced as an end in itself, which may be Dewey's own way of thinking of it. Then it is derived from a statement in C plus a statement in D according to our original pattern.)

Much of the character of a philosophy of education depends on the nature and content of the statements it includes *and makes use of* in B and D. Whether it is scientific or unscientific, naturalistic or supernaturalistic, secular or religious, idealistic, realistic, or pragmatic, rationalistic or empiricist, positivistic or metaphysical, depends entirely on what propositions it puts into B and D and makes use of in order to reach the normative conclusions in C and E. But logically, of course, just as much depends on the basic ends or principles affirmed in A, since no normative conclusions can be drawn without them. In particular, whether a position is hedonistic or non-hedonistic, utilitarian or nonutilitarian, depends entirely on the premises affirmed in A, as the case of Mill shows. Whether a philosophy of education is democratic or not also depends very largely on the ends or principles asserted in A, but probably also depends in part on what is asserted in B and D.

III. PLACING OUR AUTHORS

All of the selections in this book come from the works of four recent philosophers who have written about education—John Dewey, who is the most influential and embattled of them all, and three others: Alfred North Whitehead, Jacques Maritain, and Richard S. Peters. Some remarks must be made here by way of classifying and comparing them. On the epistemological and metaphysical basis of classification referred to earlier, philosophers of education were generally divided into three schools: idealists, realists, and pragmatists. "Idealism" is a word with several meanings but in this context it means the view (a) that all reality is mental or spiritual and (b) that to be is to be perceived or known by a mind. "Realism" too is an ambiguous term but here it stands for the view that (b) is false, that is, that objects may exist and be what they are without being perceived, known, or even thought about by a mind. Realists also usually deny (a). Pragmatism is a theory of meaning and truth; it holds (1) that the meaning of a statement is that, if we act in certain ways, certain empirical or practical consequences will take place, and (2) that a statement is true if it "works," that is, if those predicted consequences do take place when we act on it.

If we use this classification here, we must put Whitehead and Maritain down as "realists," though of different kinds, and Dewey as a "pragmatist," and we cannot classify Peters at all. No "idealist" has been included. However, this classification is no longer regarded by philosophers as being as important as the division between analytical, speculative, and normative philosophers. A speculative philosopher is one who tries to work out a full-fledged metaphysical conception of the universe as a whole and of human life and knowledge within it; a normative philosopher one who is concerned to present a systematic view of the ends, principles, or virtues by which human beings, individuals or groups, ought to live, act, and feel; and an analytical philosopher one who devotes himself to an analysis or clarification of the arguments, concepts, methods, and linguistic rules employed by human beings in their speech and thought. It is usual for speculative philosophers to do normative philosophy too, but normative thinkers do not always do speculative philosophy, and analytical philosophers typically avoid doing either speculative or normative philosophy (as well as empirical science).

In terms of this more up-to-date classification, Whitehead and Maritain are speculative philosophers; their philosophies of education are done in the context of general speculative philosophies. But they are also normative in their thinking, especially about education. Dewey is also actually a speculative philosopher of a sort, since he has a general conception of life and the world, but he usually stresses the normative function of philosophy as the most general theory for the guidance of human action and education (he sometimes defines philosophy as "the general theory of education"). Peters is primarily an analytical philosopher, though he does not entirely avoid taking normative positions in social and educational philosophy.

Among speculative philosophers, the main division is between naturalists and supernaturalists. Naturalists believe that nothing is real except what exists in time or space and can be verified by empirical methods of the kind used in every-day life and in the sciences. Supernaturalists insist that there are entities of another order, for example, a God and immortal souls, and that the universe is a purposive drama in which these entities play the leading roles. Dewey is a naturalist, as well as a pragmatist, in his general philosophy, and this shows up in his conclusions about education, though less directly than one might expect. Peters may be a naturalist too or perhaps an agnostic—it is hard to tell—but, if so, it does not manifest itself in what he says about education, though it may appear in what he does *not* say. Maritain is clearly a supernaturalist, and sets himself firmly against both naturalism and pragmatism; this appears frequently in his thoughts on education, for instance, in his stress on the cultivation of "intuition" and "faith." Indeed, in general philosophy and to some extent in philosophy of education, Maritain serves well as a representative of what Dewey is against, although he accepts many of the Deweyan reforms in education, for example, the insistence on pupil activity, manual training, and the like. Whitehead is also a supernaturalist, since he believes there is a God (though not the God of traditional theism), but this does not seem to affect his views on education very explicitly; he does speak briefly of religious education once or twice, but in such a way as to keep his tone almost entirely secular.

Talking in terms of recent controversy about education, we must say that Maritain most nearly represents the traditional position, even though he too has caught much of the spirit of "modern," "new," or "progressive" education. In fact, one reason for including him here is that he serves as an example, though not an extreme one, of the neo-aristotelian or neo-thomist line of attack on recent and especially Deweyan education taken by Robert M. Hutchins, Mortimer Adler, John D. Wild, Harry S. Broudy, and most Catholic writers. Whitehead also seems to be more traditional in his conception of subject matter in education than Dewey, and implicitly subscribes to a rather different view of the function and method of thought, but otherwise has much in common with Dewey, for example his polemic against "inert ideas," his insistence on activity, application, and use, and his view that "Life" is the one subject matter of education or that "the only use of a knowledge of the past is to equip us for the present." Peters is somewhat critical (in an essay not included here) of Dewey's vaguish talk about "experience" in education, and would surely be no less critical of Whitehead's talk about "Life" or Maritain's about "being" and "truth," but in many ways he seems to be stating views similar to Dewey's in a more analytical idiom, for instance, in what he says about aims of education or about moral education.

It is interesting to note that Dewey's stress on pupil activity and motivation in opposition to the passivity which he thought characteristic of traditional methods is echoed in one way or another by each of our other authors. This illustrates nicely Dewey's own remark that all educational reformers are given to attacking the passivity of traditional education. But, of course, our authors do not all have the same view of what activity is or of what is motivating, nor do they draw the same conclusions about what is to be done by teachers and schools. All of them would, however, be unhappy about much of what is actually being done by our schools and teachers, some at least in part because it has been too much influenced by Dewey, and Dewey himself because it has not been enough influenced by him (in *Experience and Education,* published in 1938, he complains both because so much of "the old education" still goes on and because so much of "the new education" has gone too far in the opposite direction).

We cannot try here to analyze our authors in terms of the model of a normative philosophy of education explicated earlier (that is for the student to do), but we must say something about them in relation to it. The main point to notice is that only three of them are presenting us with an explicitly normative philosophy of education—Dewey, Whitehead, and Maritain—and that none of these men uses the model in any obvious way in doing so. All three of them do, however, take the business of education to be the promotion of certain excellences of ability, habit, knowledge, trait, etc., and they give us a fairly clear idea of what these are and some thoughts about why and how they are to be promoted. Hence it should in principle be possible to analyze what they say in terms of our model. Here Dewey presents the hardest problem, because he is always critical of any such talk about basic or ultimate ends or principles as seems to be required in A. It smacks too much of the older philosophies of Plato, Aristotle, Kant, and even Mill, that he is so concerned to confute or to reconstruct. Yet, when it finally comes down to it, though he insists on "the futility of trying to establish *the* aim of education—some one final aim which subordinates all others to itself," he does subscribe at least tentatively to certain "educational aims" or "values" *within* the activity or process of education which may be used in guiding it. All he really objects to is "external ends" or "ends imposed from without," and it is not in the least clear that any of our other authors would disagree with him in this. In any case, Dewey himself sometimes speaks of "growth" or "meaning" as if it were the end or criterion *in* education in much the same spirit in which Whitehead and Maritain talk about their aims *of* education.

As for Peters, like any analytical philosopher, he is rather chary of doing normative philosophy of education, and he attacks the notion that education has aims or ends much as Dewey does, though with more analytical tools. He too objects to thinking about education as an activity or process that has an end outside itself to which it is a means. But he is nevertheless willing to speak of the "function" or "task" of the educator and of the "procedural principles" of education, and to give us some indication of what he thinks this function and these procedural principles are. Even so, his aim throughout is rather to clarify our educational thought and language than to guide our educational action; he remains the analyst rather than the mentor. In particular, he refrains from telling us how to proceed in practice, once we have our theory straight; such practical guidance he regards as the domain of the scientist and the experienced teacher. For him the job of the philosopher is to keep our theory straight and to "shed light on where empirical research needs to be done and where practical judgments have to be made," but not to do the empirical research or to make the practical judgments. Here the analytical philosopher fears to tread where our other philosophers rush in.

IV. INTRODUCING OUR AUTHORS AND SELECTIONS

The selections from our four philosophers have been divided into two groups. Part I consists mainly of essays or passages dealing with the nature and aims or principles of education in general, while Part II is chiefly made up of pieces dealing with somewhat more specific problems about the kinds, methods, programs, etc., of education. In each part there is something from each of our authors. These two groupings correspond roughly to the two parts of a normative philosophy distinguished previously, except that even the selections in the second group remain relatively general and theoretical. I should add that the divisions between the two parts are not quite clean and neat. There are some passages on the nature and aims of education in Part II and some on more specific problems in Part I. To avoid this would have meant cutting up and doing violence to pieces that were intended by their authors to be read as wholes.

Something must now be said about each set of selections in Part I. In the first set of selections Dewey discusses the nature of education and its aims and criteria. He especially attacks certain conceptions of these which he associates with traditional education. He defines education (and its end) as "growth," but is somewhat unclear as to what the criteria of growth are, though he does fasten on some excellences to be taken as aims *in* education. Indeed, as an experimentalist, he wishes to leave the question of criteria or "educational values" open for further enquiry on the basis of experience.

The essays from Whitehead included in this volume were addresses given before he came to this country, but, while they include some references to British education, were intended to have a universal validity. In the preface which precedes them Whitehead says his main idea is that "students are alive, and the purpose of education is to stimulate and guide their self-development." Elsewhere he says that the aim of education is to secure "balanced growth of individuality," a statement which is spelled out somewhat in some sentences in the essay in Part II. Given this general aim, Whitehead emphasizes in our first essay a number of excellences which education is to promote (and says a good deal about the methods to be used and the atmosphere to be provided in promoting them): discipline, culture, expert and active knowledge, living ideas, an intimate sense for the power, beauty, and structure of ideas, style, power, duty, and reverence. In the one in Part II he also stresses initiative, the sense of value, the appreciation of art, wisdom, and a "comprehension of the art of life."

The resemblances between Whitehead and Dewey are many and striking (e.g., both wish to banish what Whitehead calls "the idea of a mythical, far-off end of education"), but Whitehead was always cool toward Dewey's pragmatism, and perhaps this comes out in what follows when he distinguishes proof and utility.

In the selections in Part I Maritain first describes the nature of man, then states the aim of education, and finally spells out "the basic dispositions to be fostered," all in a straightforward fashion. There are points at which he is close to Dewey, but his supernaturalism and antipragmatism are always manifest, and more so than in Whitehead. For him, Dewey is almost wholly a disaster, and even Whitehead is too much affected by the acids of romanticism, evolutionism, and modernity. Both Dewey and Whitehead would probably think of him as one who imposes on education an external far-off end, but actually his statement about its end is not much different from theirs. The difference lies more in his view of the nature of man and of the excellences to be fostered in the course of achieving the end.

Peters does not wholly disown the enterprise of making normative judgments about education, as ·some analytical philosophers do, though he is sparing of making them. But in the essay in Part I he is doing a typical analytical job; he is analyzing and criticizing the conception (certainly present in Maritain's mind) of education as an activity or process which is a means to an end or result beyond itself, and arguing that so-called "values" come into education, not as ends, but as "procedural principles." He is, however, willing to lay down some procedural principles, especially in the essay in

Part II, and even to say that an educator has a certain function or task, in spite of his impatience "with the endless talk about the aims of education."

I shall also give here an introduction to the readings in Part II. This part consists of selections in which our four authors lay down general guidelines for thinking about questions of method, subject-matter, and program in education, intellectual and moral. Here especially I must stress the fact that the selections are incomplete; they give only samples of our authors' reflections on such questions, and must not be taken as doing anything more, particularly in the case of Dewey.

For Dewey the business of education is to promote growth—the living of "a life which is fruitful and inherently significant." This means it must provide both interest and discipline, and in the first passage Dewey explains how it may do both. But growth mainly depends on increased control and perception of meaning in experience and this involves acquiring the ability and habit of thinking and acting intelligently or scientifically in all situations and on all matters. Hence Dewey argues in the second selection that *the* method of intellectual education is to "exact, promote, and test" such thinking, and then explains what this means for the teacher and the schools. These passages should show how he would answer the critics who say he neglects discipline of mind in favor of adjustment and motivation. Growth also has an appreciative or enjoyable aspect, however, which Dewey emphasizes in the third selection. I quote it partly to show that, although he is a pragmatist and often rejects the means-ends distinction, he does still believe in intrinsic values and their appreciation. He even finds here an important place for art, much as both Whitehead and Maritain do. In general, however, he believes that both thinking and appreciation may and should be taught in all "subjects," and opposes the usual distinction of subjects and the assumption that different subjects promote different values or excellences. Thus, in the last passage, he breaks down the distinction between intellectual and moral education by contending that the same program that teaches thinking, rightly carried out, will also foster the moral excellences required for individual growth and democratic social life.

Whitehead says in his preface that he is mainly concerned about intellectual education, and his main point in the essay that follows is to sketch an interesting conception of the program and stages of intellectual education, but he also says a little about morality and religion, and ends by emphasizing the importance of aesthetic education. Throughout, it is instructive to notice how his views resemble and differ from Dewey's on the place of interest and discipline, the nature of thinking and subject matter, and the role of appreciation and intrinsic values.

Maritain keeps the distinctions between theoretical and practical reason and between intellectual and moral education that Dewey rejects. In the first passages quoted he writes about the role of the teacher and lays down four rules to be followed. Then comes a passage on the curriculum and another on the stages of education. The latter is interesting to compare with what Whitehead says. Throughout he indicates what he regards as true and false in "contemporary education." His insistence on the supernatural dimension is clear, as is his opposition to Dewey, who, he thinks, wrongly exalts intelligence and thinking over knowledge and truth. He also separates subject matter into formal subjects and assigns them different functions and values—something Dewey always opposes. In the last group of passages Maritain first relates intellectual and moral education and then discusses the latter; and here especially he contends that there are excellences which cannot be taught and must be given by God in grace.

Maritain mentions a "paradox" of education, and, in the essay included here, Peters addresses himself to another one. He states and discusses it mainly in terms of moral education, but it is clear that he regards it as a problem of all education which initiates the young into "worthwhile activities." The problem is that education must promote rational autonomy *and* also the formation of habits of mind and character—all of our philosophers are agreed on this. Indeed, the latter is a condition of the achievement of the former. We acquire an excellence (or "language") by acquiring a habit of acting in a certain way (or being initiated into its "literature"). Yet it seems that the methods to be used in education must defeat the goal. Peters' answer is that everything depends on how habits are conceived and "at what age and in what manner such habits are formed." Here he is close to Dewey, though he insists on remaining "theoretical" or analytical, in a way in which Dewey would not.

In these paragraphs I have brought out some agreements and differences between our authors, and there are others. The point, however, is not merely to show what these are. Rather, it is to help the student to see what he may take to be agreed on and what he must reflect on further and make up his own mind about.

V. ENVOI

Now a final word is needed about the spirit in which this book should be studied. The point of philosophy, as Socrates said, is that we may lead examined and intelligent lives; the point of doing philosophy of education is to do our educating and being educated, which is going on most of our lives, in an examined and intelligent way. As Dr. Conant, Admiral Rickover, and others have been pointing out, we must all be concerned about education and what goes on in our schools—citizens and parents as well as administrators and teachers. This means thinking carefully, informedly, and philosophically about it. The point of this book, accordingly, is not merely to acquaint the reader with the views of our four authors, nor is it to encourage him to be an eclectic in his thinking about education, as too many introductions to educational philosophy do. It is to help him, through a study of the thought of others, to reach an examined and intelligent position of his own.

PART I

Education, Its Nature, Aims and Principles

JOHN DEWEY

Education as Growth

John Dewey (1859–1952). Whitehead once said, "We are living in the midst of the period subject to Dewey's influence," and this is certainly true as far as education is concerned. Yet it is unfair to attribute all that is good or all that is bad in American education today to Dewey, as his followers and critics, respectively, often do. For one thing, his influence has not been that complete; for another, he did not advocate all that has been attributed to him.

Dewey was born in Vermont, educated at the University of Vermont and Johns Hopkins, and taught philosophy at Michigan, Chicago, and Columbia. After college he taught briefly in public schools and at Chicago was director of a famous experimental school. All during his career he wrote a great deal both about education and about philosophy, and his theory of education was closer to the center of his philosophy than is usually the case. He was one of our greatest philosophers in general, and has been called the greatest philosopher of education since Plato, not without reason. Though for drastic reform in education, he was critical all along of so-called "progressive education," holding to a more careful line of his own, which, it must be admitted, he did not always express as carefully as he should have.

Reprinted with permission of the publisher from *Democracy and Education* by John Dewey. Copyright 1916 by The Macmillan Company, renewed 1944 by John Dewey. [Taken from the paperbound edition (1961), pp. 49–53, 76–80, 243–244, 359, *passim.*]

We have been occupied with the conditions and implications of growth. If our conclusions are justified, they carry with them, however, definite educational consequences. When it is said that education is development, everything depends upon *how* development is conceived. Our net conclusion is that life is development, and that developing, growing, is life. Translated into its educational equivalents, that means (*i*) that the educational process has no end beyond itself; it is its own end; and that (*ii*) the educational process is one of continual reorganizing, reconstructing, transforming. . . .

Three ideas which have been criticized, namely, the merely privative nature of immaturity, static adjustment to a fixed environment, and rigidity of habit, are all connected with a false idea of growth or development,—that it is a movement toward a fixed goal. Growth is regarded as *having* an end, instead of *being* an end. The educational counterparts of the three fallacious ideas are first, failure to take account of the instinctive or native powers of the young; secondly, failure to develop initiative in coping with novel situations; thirdly, an undue emphasis upon drill and other devices which secure automatic skill at the expense of personal perception. In all cases, the adult environment is accepted as a standard for the child. He is to be brought up *to* it. . . .

Since in reality there is nothing to which growth is relative save more growth, there is nothing to which education is subordinate save more education. It is a commonplace to say that education should not cease when one leaves school. The point of this commonplace is that the purpose of school education is to insure the continuance of education by organizing the powers that insure growth. The inclination to learn from life itself and to make the conditions of life such that all will learn in the process of living is the finest product of schooling.

When we abandon the attempt to define immaturity by means of fixed comparison with adult accomplishments, we are compelled to give up thinking of it as denoting lack of desired traits . . . we are also forced to surrender our habit of thinking of instruction as a method of supplying this lack by pouring knowledge into a mental and moral hole which awaits filling. Since life means growth, a living creature lives as truly and positively at one stage as at another, with the same intrinsic fullness and the same absolute claims. Hence education means the enterprise of supplying the conditions which insure growth, or adequacy of life, irrespective of age. . . .

Realization that life is growth protects us from that so-called idealizing of childhood which in effect is nothing but lazy indulgence. Life is not to be identified with every superficial act and interest. Even though it is not always easy to tell whether what appears to be mere surface fooling is a sign of some nascent as yet untrained power, we must remember that manifestations are not to be accepted as ends in themselves. They are signs of possible growth. They are to be turned into means of development, of carrying power forward, not indulged or cultivated for their own sake. Excessive attention to surface phenomena (even in the way of rebuke as well as of encouragement) may lead to their fixation and thus to arrested development. What impulses are moving toward, not what they have been, is the important thing for parent and teacher. . . .

Power to grow depends upon need for others and plasticity. Both of these conditions are at their height in childhood and youth. Plasticity or the power to learn from experience means the formation of habits. Habits give control over the environment, power to utilize it for human purposes. Habits take the form both of habituation, or a general and persistent balance of organic activities with the surroundings, and of active capacities to readjust activity to meet new conditions. The former furnishes the background of growth; the latter constitute growing. Active habits involve thought, invention, and initiative in applying capacities to new aims. They are opposed to routine which marks an arrest of growth. Since growth is the characteristic of life, education is all one with growing; it has no end beyond itself. The criterion of the value of school education is the extent in which it creates a desire for continued growth and supplies means for making the desire effective in fact. . . .

In its contrast with the ideas both of unfolding of latent powers from within, and of the formation from without, whether by physical nature or by the cultural products of the past, the ideal of growth results in the conception that education is a constant reorganizing or reconstructing of experience. It has all the time an immediate end, and so far as activity is educative, it reaches that end—the direct transformation of the quality of experience. Infancy, youth, adult life,—all stand on the same educative level in the sense that what is really *learned* at any and every stage of experience constitutes the value of that experience, and in the sense that it is the chief business of life at every point to make living thus contribute to an enrichment of its own perceptible meaning.

We thus reach a technical definition of education: It is that reconstruction or reorganization of experience which adds to the meaning of experience, and which increases ability to direct the course of subsequent experience. (1) The increment of meaning corresponds to the increased perception of the connections and continuities of the activities in which we are engaged. The activity begins in an impulsive form; that is, it is blind. It does not know what it is about; that is to say, what are its interactions with other activities. An activity which brings education or instruction with it makes one aware of some of the connections which had been imperceptible. To recur to our simple example, a child who reaches for a bright light gets burned. Henceforth he *knows* that a certain act of touching in connection with a certain act of vision (and *vice-versa*) means heat and pain; or, a certain light means a source of heat. The acts by which a scientific man in his laboratory learns more about flame differ no whit in principle. By doing certain things, he makes perceptible certain connections of heat with other things, which had been previously ignored. Thus his acts in relation to these things get more meaning; he knows better what he is doing or "is about" when he has to do with them; he can *intend* consequences instead of just letting them happen—all synonymous ways of saying the same thing. At the same stroke, the flame has gained in meaning; all that is known about combustion, oxidation, about light and temperature, may become an intrinsic part of its intellectual content.

(2) The other side of an educative experience is an added power of subsequent direction or control. To say that one knows what he is about, or can intend certain consequences, is to say, of course, that he can better anticipate what is going to happen; that he can, therefore, get ready or prepare in advance so as to secure beneficial consequences and avert undesirable ones. A genuinely educative experience, then, one in which instruction is conveyed and ability increased, is contradistinguished from a routine activity on one hand, and a capricious activity on the other. (*a*) In the latter one "does not care what happens"; one just lets himself go and avoids connecting the consequences of one's act (the evidences of its connections with other things) with the act. It is customary to frown upon such aimless random activity, treating it as willful mischief or carelessness or lawlessness. But there is a tendency to seek the cause of such aimless activities in the youth's own disposition, isolated from everything else. But in fact such activity is explosive, and due to

maladjustment with surroundings. Individuals act capriciously whenever they act under external dictation, or from being told, without having a purpose of their own or perceiving the bearing of the deed upon other acts. One may learn by doing something which he does not understand; even in the most intelligent action, we do much which we do not mean, because the largest portion of the connections of the act we consciously intend are not perceived or anticipated. But we learn only because after the act is performed we note results which we had not noted before. But much work in school consists in setting up rules by which pupils are to act of such a sort that even after pupils have acted, they are not led to see the connection between the result—say the answer—and the method pursued. So far as they are concerned, the whole thing is a trick and a kind of miracle. Such action is essentially capricious, and leads to capricious habits. (*b*) Routine action, action which is automatic, may increase skill to do a *particular* thing. In so far, it might be said to have an educative effect. But it does not lead to new perceptions of bearings and connections; it limits rather than widens the meaning-horizon. And since the environment changes and our way of acting has to be modified in order successfully to keep a balanced connection with things, an isolated uniform way of acting becomes disastrous at some critical moment. The vaunted "skill" turns out gross ineptitude.

The essential contrast of the idea of education as continuous reconstruction with the other one-sided conceptions which have been criticized in this and the previous chapter is that it identifies the end (the result) and the process. This is verbally self-contradictory, but only verbally. It means that experience as an active process occupies time and that its later period completes its earlier portion; it brings to light connections involved, but hitherto unperceived. The later outcome thus reveals the meaning of the earlier, while the experience as a whole establishes a bent or disposition toward the things possessing this meaning. Every such continuous experience or activity is educative, and all education resides in having such experiences.

It remains only to point out . . . that the reconstruction of experience may be social as well as personal. For purposes of simplification we have spoken in the earlier chapters somewhat as if the education of the immature which fills them with the spirit of the social group to which they belong, were a sort of catching up of the child with the aptitudes and resources of the adult group. In static societies,

societies which make the maintenance of established custom their measure of value, this conception applies in the main. But not in progressive communities. They endeavor to shape the experiences of the young so that instead of reproducing current habits, better habits shall be formed, and thus the future adult society be an improvement on their own. Men have long had some intimation of the extent to which education may be consciously used to eliminate obvious social evils through starting the young on paths which shall not produce these ills, and some idea of the extent in which education may be made an instrument of realizing the better hopes of men. But we are doubtless far from realizing the potential efficacy of education as a constructive agency of improving society, from realizing that it represents not only a development of children and youth but also of the future society of which they will be the constituents. . . .

A narrow and moralistic view of morals is responsible for the failure to recognize that all the aims and values which are desirable in education are themselves moral. Discipline, natural development, culture, social efficiency, are moral traits—marks of a person who is a worthy member of that society which it is the business of education to further. There is an old saying to the effect that it is not enough for a man to be good; he must be good for something. The something for which a man must be good is capacity to live as a social member so that what he gets from living with others balances with what he contributes. What he gets and gives as a human being, a being with desires, emotions, and ideas, is not external possessions, but a widening and deepening of conscious life—a more intense, disciplined, and expanding realization of meanings. What he *materially* receives and gives is at most opportunities and means for the evolution of conscious life. Otherwise, it is neither giving nor taking, but a shifting about of the position of things in space, like the stirring of water and sand with a stick. Discipline, culture, social efficiency, personal refinement, improvement of character are but phases of the growth of capacity nobly to share in such a balanced experience. And education is not a mere means to such a life. Education is such a life. To maintain capacity for such education is the essence of morals. For conscious life is a continual beginning afresh. . . .

It is of course possible to classify in a general way the various valuable phases of life. In order to get a survey of aims sufficiently wide . . . to give breadth and flexibility to the enterprise of education, there is some advantage in such a classification. But it is a great mistake to regard these values as ultimate ends to which the concrete satisfactions of experience are subordinate. They are nothing but generalizations, more or less adequate, of concrete goods. Health, wealth, efficiency, sociability, utility, culture, happiness itself are only abstract terms which sum up a multitude of particulars. To regard such things as standards for the valuation of concrete topics and process of education is to subordinate to an abstraction the concrete facts from which the abstraction is derived. They are not in any true sense standards of valuation; these are found . . . in the *specific realizations* which form tastes and habits of preference. They are, however, of significance as points of view elevated above the details of life whence to survey the field and see how its constituent details are distributed, and whether they are well proportioned.

No classification can have other than a provisional validity. The following may prove of some help. We may say that the kind of experience to which the work of the schools should contribute is one marked by executive competency in the management of resources and obstacles encountered (efficiency); by sociability, or interest in the direct companionship of others; by aesthetic taste or capacity to appreciate artistic excellence in at least some of its classic forms; by trained intellectual method, or interest in some mode of scientific achievement; and by sensitiveness to the rights and claims of others—conscientiousness. And while these considerations are not standards of value, they are useful criteria for survey, criticism, and better organization of existing methods and subject matter of instruction.

ALFRED NORTH WHITEHEAD

The Aims of Education

*Alfred North Whitehead (1861–1947) ranks as one of the great mathe-
matical logicians and speculative philosophers of recent times. He was
born in England and died in the United States. Before 1924 he taught
mathematics at Cambridge and in London; after that he taught philosophy at Harvard until 1937. Throughout he had much occasion to be concerned with education, liberal and technical, and his reflections on it have
been widely read and quoted, for, except in his more technical writings,
he was eminently readable and quotable. To use his own word, his
thought had "style," whatever its subject matter.*

Culture is activity of thought, and receptiveness to beauty and
humane feeling. Scraps of information have nothing to do with it.
A merely well-informed man is the most useless bore on God's
earth. What we should aim at producing is men who possess both
culture and expert knowledge in some special direction. Their expert
knowledge will give them the ground to start from, and their culture
will lead them as deep as philosophy and as high as art. We have
to remember that the valuable intellectual development is self-
development, and that it mostly takes place between the ages of
sixteen and thirty. As to training, the most important part is given
by mothers before the age of twelve. . . .

In training a child to activity of thought, above all things we
must beware of what I will call "inert ideas"—that is to say, ideas
that are merely received into the mind without being utilised, or
tested, or thrown into fresh combinations.

Let us now ask how in our system of education we are to guard
against this mental dryrot. We enunciate two educational command-
ments, "Do not teach too many subjects," and again, "What you
teach, teach thoroughly."

The result of teaching small parts of a large number of subjects
is the passive reception of disconnected ideas, not illumined with

any spark of vitality. Let the main ideas which are introduced into a child's education be few and important, and let them be thrown into every combination possible. The child should make them his own, and should understand their application here and now in the circumstances of his actual life. From the very beginning of his education, the child should experience the joy of discovery. The discovery which he has to make, is that general ideas give an understanding of that stream of events which pours through his life, which is his life. By understanding I mean more than a mere logical analysis, though that is included. I mean "understanding" in the sense in which it is used in the French proverb, "To understand all, is to forgive all." Pedants sneer at an education which is useful. But if education is not useful, what is it? Is it a talent, to be hidden away in a napkin? Of course, education should be useful, whatever your aim in life. It was useful to Saint Augustine and it was useful to Napoleon. It is useful, because understanding is useful.

I pass lightly over that understanding which should be given by the literary side of education. Nor do I wish to be supposed to pronounce on the relative merits of a classical or a modern curriculum. I would only remark that the understanding which we want is an understanding of an insistent present. The only use of a knowledge of the past is to equip us for the present. No more deadly harm can be done to young minds than by depreciation of the present. The present contains all that there is. It is holy ground; for it is the past, and it is the future. . . .

Passing now to the scientific and logical side of education, we remember that here also ideas which are not utilised are positively harmful. By utilising an idea, I mean relating it to that stream, compounded of sense perceptions, feelings, hopes, desires, and of mental activities adjusting thought to thought, which forms our life. I can imagine a set of beings which might fortify their souls by passively reviewing disconnected ideas. Humanity is not built that way —except perhaps some editors of newspapers.

In scientific training, the first thing to do with an idea is to prove it. But allow me for one moment to extend the meaning of "prove"; I mean—to prove its worth. Now an idea is not worth much unless the propositions in which it is embodied are true. Accordingly an essential part of the proof of an idea is the proof, either by experiment or by logic, of the truth of the propositions. But it is not essential that this proof of the truth should constitute the first introduction to the idea. After all, its assertion by the authoriy of respectable teachers is sufficient evidence to begin with. In our first contact with a set of propositions, we commence by appreciating their importance. That is what we all do in after-life. We do not attempt, in the strict sense, to prove or to disprove anything, unless its importance makes it worthy of that honour. These two processes of proof, in the narrow sense, and of appreciation, do not require a rigid separation in time. Both can be proceeded with nearly concurrently. But in so far as either process must have the priority, it should be that of appreciation by use.

Furthermore, we should not endeavour to use propositions in isolation. Emphatically I do not mean, a neat little set of experiments to illustrate Proposition I and then the proof of Proposition I, a neat little set of experiments to illustrate Proposition II and then the proof of Proposition II, and so on to the end of the book. Nothing could be more boring. Interrelated truths are utilised *en bloc,* and the various propositions are employed in any order, and with any reiteration. Choose some important applications of your theoretical subject; and study them concurrently with the systematic theoretical exposition. Keep the theoretical exposition short and simple, but let it be strict and rigid so far as it goes. It should not be too long for it to be easily known with thoroughness and accuracy. The consequences of a plethora of half-digested theoretical knowledge are deplorable. Also the theory should not be muddled up with the practice. The child should have no doubt when it is proving and when it is utilising. My point is that what is proved should be utilised, and that what is utilised should—so far as is practicable—be proved. I am far from asserting that proof and utilisation are the same thing. . . .

Education is the acquisition of the art of the utilisation of knowledge. This is an art very difficult to impart. Whenever a text-book is written of real educational worth, you may be quite certain that some reviewer will say that it will be difficult to teach from it. Of course it will be difficult to teach from it. If it were easy, the book ought to be burned; for it cannot be educational. In education, as elsewhere, the broad primrose path leads to a nasty place. . . .

We now return to my previous point, that theoretical ideas should always find important applications within the pupil's curriculum. This is not an easy doctrine to apply, but a very hard one. It contains within itself the problem of keeping knowledge alive, of preventing it from becoming inert, which is the central problem of all education.

The best procedure will depend on several factors, none of which can be neglected, namely, the genius of the teacher, the intellectual type of the pupils, their prospects in life, the opportunities offered by the immediate surroundings of the school, and allied factors of this sort. It is for this reason that the uniform external examination is so deadly. We do not denounce it because we are cranks, and like denouncing established things. We are not so childish. Also, of course, such examinations have their use in testing slackness. Our reason of dislike is very definite and very practical. It kills the best part of culture. When you analyse in the light of experience the central task of education, you find that its successful accomplishment depends on a delicate adjustment of many variable factors. The reason is that we are dealing with human minds, and not with dead matter. The evocation of curiosity, of judgment, of the power of mastering a complicated tangle of circumstances, the use of theory in giving foresight in special cases—all these powers are not to be imparted by a set rule embodied in one schedule of examination subjects.

I appeal to you, as practical teachers. With good discipline, it is always possible to pump into the minds of a class a certain quantity of inert knowledge. You take a text-book and make them learn it. So far, so good. The child then knows how to solve a quadratic equation. But what is the point of teaching a child to solve a quadratic equation? There is a traditional answer to this question. It runs thus: The mind is an instrument, you first sharpen it, and then use it; the acquisition of the power of solving a quadratic equation is part of the process of sharpening the mind. Now there is just enough truth in this answer to have made it live through the ages. But for all its half-truth, it embodies a radical error which bids fair to stifle the genius of the modern world. . . . The mind is never passive; it is a perpetual activity, delicate, receptive, responsive to stimulus. You cannot postpone its life until you have sharpened it. Whatever interest attaches to your subject-matter must be evoked here and now; whatever powers you are strengthening in the pupil, must be exercised here and now; whatever possibilities of mental life your teaching should impart, must be exhibited here and now. That is the golden rule of education, and a very difficult rule to follow.

The difficulty is just this: the apprehension of general ideas, intellectual habits of mind, and pleasurable interest in mental achievement can be evoked by no form of words, however accurately adjusted. All practical teachers know that education is a patient process of the mastery of details, minute by minute, hour by hour, day by day. There is no royal road to learning through an airy path of brilliant generalisations. There is a proverb about the difficulty of seeing the wood because of the trees. That difficulty is exactly the point which I am enforcing. The problem of education is to make the pupil see the wood by means of the trees.

The solution which I am urging, is to eradicate the fatal disconnection of subjects which kills the vitality of our modern curriculum. There is only one subject-matter for education, and that is Life in all its manifestations. Instead of this single unity, we offer children— Algebra, from which nothing follows; Geometry, from which nothing follows; Science, from which nothing follows; History, from which nothing follows; a Couple of Languages, never mastered; and lastly, most dreary of all, Literature, represented by plays of Shakespeare, with philological notes and short analyses of plot and character to be in substance committed to memory. Can such a list be said to represent Life, as it is known in the midst of the living of it? The best that can be said of it is, that it is a rapid table of contents which a deity might run over in his mind while he was thinking of creating a world, and had not yet determined how to put it together.

Let us now return to quadratic equations. We still have on hand the unanswered question. Why should children be taught their solution? Unless quadratic equations fit into a connected curriculum, of course, there is no reason to teach anything about them. Furthermore, extensive as should be the place of mathematics in a complete culture, I am a little doubtful whether for many types of boys algebraic solutions of quadratic equations do not lie on the specialist side of mathematics. I may here remind you that as yet I have not said anything of the psychology or the content of the specialism, which is so necessary a part of an ideal education. But all that is an evasion of our real question, and I merely state it in order to avoid being misunderstood in my answer.

Quadratic equations are part of algebra, and algebra is the intellectual instrument which has been created for rendering clear the quantitative aspects of the world. There is no getting out of it. Through and through the world is infected with quantity. To talk sense, is to talk in quantities. It is no use saying that the nation is large,—How large? It is no use saying that radium is scarce,—How scarce? You cannot evade quantity. You may fly to poetry and to music, and quantity and number will face you in your rhythms and your octaves. Elegant intellects which despise the theory of quantity, are but half developed. They are more to be pitied than blamed. The scraps of gibberish, which in their school-days were taught to them in the name of algebra, deserve some contempt.

This question of the degeneration of algebra into gibberish, both in word and in fact, affords a pathetic instance of the uselessness of reforming educational schedules without a clear conception of the attributes which you wish to evoke in the living minds of the children. A few years ago there was an outcry that school algebra was in need of reform, but there was a general agreement that graphs would put everything right. So all sorts of things were extruded, and graphs were introduced. So far as I can see, with no sort of idea behind them, but just graphs. Now every examination paper has one or two questions on graphs. Personally, I am an enthusiastic adherent of graphs. But I wonder whether as yet we have gained very much. You cannot put life into any schedule of general education unless you succeed in exhibiting its relation to some essential characteristic of all intelligent or emotional perception. It is a hard saying, but it is true; and I do not see how to make it any easier. In making these little formal alterations you are beaten by the very nature of things. You are pitted against too skilful an adversary, who will see to it that the pea is always under the other thimble.

Reformation must begin at the other end. First, you must make up your mind as to those quantitive aspects of the world which are simple enough to be introduced into general education; then a schedule of algebra should be framed which will about find its exemplification in these applications. We need not fear for our pet graphs, they will be there in plenty when we once begin to treat algebra as a serious means of studying the world. Some of the simplest applications will be found in the quantities which occur in the simplest study of society. The curves of history are more vivid and more informing than the dry catalogues of names and dates which comprise the greater part of that arid school study. What purpose is effected by a catalogue of undistinguished kings and queens? Tom, Dick, or Harry, they are all dead. General resurrections are failures, and are better postponed. The quantitative flux of the forces of modern society is capable of very simple exhibition. Meanwhile, the ideas of the variable, of the function, of rate of change, of equations and their solution, of elimination, are being studied as an abstract science for their own sake. Not, of course, in the pompous phrases with which I am alluding to them, here, but with that iteration of simple special cases proper to teaching.

If this course be followed, the route from Chaucer to the Black Death, from the Black Death to modern Labour troubles, will connect the tales of the mediæval pilgrims with the abstract science of algebra, both yielding diverse aspects of that single theme, Life. . . .

I must beg you to remember what I have been insisting on above. In the first place, one train of thought will not suit all groups of children. For example, I should expect that artisan children will want something more concrete and, in a sense, swifter than I have set down here. Perhaps I am wrong, but that is what I should guess. In the second place, I am not contemplating one beautiful lecture stimulating, once and for all, an admiring class. That is not the way in which education proceeds. No; all the time the pupils are hard at work solving examples, drawing graphs, and making experiments, until they have a thorough hold on the whole subject. I am describing the interspersed explanations, the directions which should be given to their thoughts. The pupils have got to be made to feel that they are studying something, and are not merely executing intellectual minuets.

Finally, if you are teaching pupils for some general examination, the problem of sound teaching is greatly complicated. Have you ever noticed the zig-zag moulding round a Norman arch? The ancient work is beautiful, the modern work is hideous. The reason is, that the modern work is done to exact measure, the ancient work is varied according to the idiosyncrasy of the workman. Here it is crowded, and there it is expanded. Now the essence of getting pupils through examinations is to give equal weight to all parts of the schedule. But mankind is naturally specialist. One man sees a whole subject, where another can find only a few detached examples. I know that it seems contradictory to allow for specialism in a curriculum especially designed for a broad culture. Without contradictions the world would be simpler, and perhaps duller. But I am certain that in education wherever you exclude specialism you destroy life.

We now come to the other great branch of a general mathematical education, namely Geometry. The same principles apply. The theoretical part should be clear-cut, rigid, short, and important. Every proposition not absolutely necessary to exhibit the main connection of ideas should be cut out, but the great fundamental ideas should be all there. No omission of concepts, such as those of Similarity and Proportion. We must remember that, owing to the aid rendered by the visual presence of a figure, Geometry is a field of unequalled excellence for the exercise of the deductive faculties of reasoning. Then, of course, there follows Geometrical Drawing, with its training for the hand and eye.

But, like Algebra, Geometry and Geometrical Drawing must be extended beyond the mere circle of geometrical ideas. In an industrial neighbourhood, machinery and workshop practice form the appropriate extension. For example, in the London Polytechnics this has been achieved with conspicuous success. For many secondary schools I suggest that surveying and maps are the natural applications. In particular, plane-table surveying should lead pupils to a vivid apprehension of the immediate application of geometric truths. Simple drawing apparatus, a surveyor's chain, and a surveyor's compass, should enable the pupils to rise from the survey and mensuration of a field to the construction of the map of a small district. The best education is to be found in gaining the utmost information from the simplest apparatus. The provision of elaborate instruments is greatly to be deprecated. To have constructed the map of a small district, to have considered its roads, its contours, its geology, its climate, its relation to other districts, the effects on the status of its inhabitants, will teach more history and geography than any knowledge of Perkin Warbeck or of Behren's Straits. I mean not a nebulous lecture on the subject, but a serious investigation in which the real facts are definitely ascertained by the aid of accurate theoretical knowledge. A typical mathematical problem should be: Survey such and such a field, draw a plan of it to such and such a scale, and find the area. It would be quite a good procedure to impart the necessary geometrical propositions without their proofs. Then, concurrently in the same term, the proofs of the propositions would be learnt while the survey was being made.

Fortunately, the specialist side of education presents an easier problem than does the provision of a general culture. For this there are many reasons. One is that many of the principles of procedure to be observed are the same in both cases, and it is unnecessary to recapitulate. Another reason is that specialist training takes place—or should take place—at a more advanced stage of the pupil's course, and thus there is easier material to work upon. But undoubtedly the chief reason is that the specialist study is normally a study of peculiar interest to the student. He is studying it because, for some reason, he wants to know it. This makes all the difference. The general culture is designed to foster an activity of mind; the specialist course utilises this activity. But it does not do to lay too much stress on these neat antitheses. As we have already seen, in the general course foci of special interest will arise; and similarly in the special study, the external connexions of the subject drag thought outwards.

Again, there is not one course of study which merely gives general culture, and another which gives special knowledge. The subjects pursued for the sake of a general education are special subjects specially studied; and, on the other hand, one of the ways of encouraging general mental activity is to foster a special devotion. You may not divide the seamless coat of learning. What education has to impart is an intimate sense for the power of ideas, for the beauty of ideas, and for the structure of ideas, together with a particular body of knowledge which has peculiar reference to the life of the being possessing it.

The appreciation of the structure of ideas is that side of a cultured mind which can only grow under the influence of a special study. I mean that eye for the whole chessboard, for the bearing of one set of ideas on another. Nothing but a special study can give any appreciation for the exact formulation of general ideas, for their relations when formulated, for their service in the comprehension of life. A mind so disciplined should be both more abstract and more concrete. It has been trained in the comprehension of abstract thought and in the analysis of facts.

Finally, there should grow the most austere of all mental qualities; I mean the sense for style. It is an æsthetic sense, based on admiration for the direct attainment of a foreseen end, simply and without waste. Style in art, style in literature, style in science, style in logic, style in practical execution have fundamentally the same æsthetic qualities, namely, attainment and restraint. The love of a subject in itself and for itself, where it is not the sleepy pleasure of pacing a mental quarter-deck, is the love of style as manifested in that study.

Here we are brought back to the position from which we started, the utility of education. Style, in its finest sense, is the last acquirement of the educated mind; it is also the most useful. It pervades the whole being. The administrator with a sense for style hates waste; the engineer with a sense for style economises his material; the artisan with a sense for style prefers good work. Style is the ultimate morality of mind.

But above style, and above knowledge, there is something, a vague shape like fate above the Greek gods. That something is Power. Style is the fashioning of power, the restraining of power. But, after all, the power of attainment of the desired end is fundamental. The first thing is to get there. Do not bother about your style, but solve your problem, justify the ways of God to man, administer your province, or do whatever else is set before you.

Where, then, does style help? In this, with style the end is attained without side issues, without raising undesirable inflammations. With style you attain your end and nothing but your end. With style the effect of your activity is calculable, and foresight is the last gift of gods to men. With style your power is increased, for your mind is not distracted with irrelevancies, and you are more likely to attain your object. Now style is the exclusive privilege of the expert. Whoever heard of the style of an amateur painter, of the style of an amateur poet? Style is always the product of specialist study, the peculiar contribution of specialism to culture.

English education in its present phase suffers from a lack of definite aim, and from an external machinery which kills its vitality. Hitherto in this address I have been considering the aims which should govern education. In this respect England halts between two opinions. It has not decided whether to produce amateurs or experts. The profound change in the world which the nineteenth century has produced is that the growth of knowledge has given foresight. The amateur is essentially a man with appreciation and with immense versatility in mastering a given routine. But he lacks the foresight which comes from special knowledge. The object of this address is to suggest how to produce the expert without loss of the essential virtues of the amateur. . . .

When one considers in its length and in its breadth the importance of this question of the education of a nation's young, the broken lives, the defeated hopes, the national failures, which result from the frivolous inertia with which it is treated, it is difficult to restrain within oneself a savage rage. In the conditions of modern life the rule is absolute, the race which does not value trained intelligence is doomed. Not all your heroism, not all your social charm, not all your wit, not all your victories on land or at sea, can move back the finger of fate. To-day we maintain ourselves. To-morrow science will have moved forward yet one more step, and there will be no appeal from the judgment which will then be pronounced on the uneducated.

We can be content with no less than the old summary of educational ideal which has been current at any time from the dawn of our civilisation. The essence of education is that it be religious.

Pray, what is religious education?

A religious education is an education which inculcates duty and reverence. Duty arises from our potential control over the course of events. Where attainable knowledge could have changed the issue, ignorance has the guilt of vice. And the foundation of reverence is this perception, that the present holds within itself the complete sum of existence, backwards and forwards, that whole amplitude of time, which is eternity.

JACQUES MARITAIN

Man's Nature and the Aims
of His Education

Jacques Maritain (1882–   ), first a follower of Henri Bergson in philosophy, later embraced Catholicism and Thomism and became one of the outstanding philosophical interpreters of Catholic neo-scholasticism, first in France and, after 1940, in this country. He taught at the Institut Catholique in Paris, at Columbia, and at Princeton, retiring in 1953. His many writings cover the whole range of philosophy, including the philosophy of education. Always putting old wine into new bags, he is at once both modern and orthodox in his views on education.

[THE NATURE OF MAN]

The educational task is both greater and more mysterious and, in a sense, humbler than many imagine. If the aim of education is the helping and guiding of man toward his own human achievement, education cannot escape the problems and entanglements of philosophy, for it supposes by its very nature a philosophy of man, and from the outset it is obliged to answer the question: "What is man?" which the philosophical sphinx is asking.

I should like to observe at this point that, definitely speaking, there are only two classes or categories of notions concerning man which play fair, so to speak: the purely scientific idea of man and the philosophical-religious one. According to its genuine methodological type, the scientific idea of man, like every idea recast by strictly experimental science, gets rid as far as possible of any ontological content, so that it may be entirely verifiable in sense-experience. On this point the most recent theorists of science, the neopositivists of the school of Vienna, are quite right. The purely scientific idea of man tends only to link together measurable and observable data taken as such, and is determined from the very start not to consider anything like being or essence, not to answer any question like: Is there a soul or isn't there? Does the spirit exist

From Jacques Maritain, *Education at the Crossroads* (New Haven: Yale University Press, 1943). Used by permission of Yale University Press. [Taken from the paperbound edition (1960), pp. 4–7, 10–15, 17–18, 36–38.]

or only matter? Is there freedom or determinism? Purpose or chance? Value or simple fact? For such questions are out of the realm of science. The purely scientific idea of man is, and must be, a phenomenalized idea without reference to ultimate reality.[1]

The philosophical-religious idea of man, on the contrary, is an ontological idea. It is not entirely verifiable in sense-experience, though it possesses criteria and proofs of its own, and it deals with the essential and intrinsic, though not visible or tangible characters, and with the intelligible density of that being which we call man.

Now it is obvious that the purely scientific idea of man can provide us with invaluable and ever-growing information concerning the means and tools of education, but by itself it can neither primarily found nor primarily guide education, for education needs primarily to know what man *is*, what is the nature of man and the scale of values it essentially involves; and the purely scientific idea of man, because it ignores "being-as-such," does not know such things, but only what emerges from the human being in the realm of sense observation and measurement. . . .

Thus the fact remains that the complete and integral idea of man which is the prerequisite of education can only be a philosophical and religious idea of man. I say philosophical, because this idea pertains to the nature or essence of man; I say religious, because of the existential status of this human nature in relation to God and the special gifts and trials and vocation involved. . . .

In answer to our question, then, "What is man?" we may give the Greek, Jewish, and the Christian idea of man: man as an animal endowed with reason, whose supreme dignity is in the intellect; and man as a free individual in personal relation with God, whose supreme righteousness consists in voluntarily obeying the law of God; and man as a sinful and wounded creature called to divine life and to the freedom of grace, whose supreme perfection consists of love. . . .

[THE AIM OF EDUCATION]

We may now define in a more precise manner the aim of education. It is to guide man in the evolving dynamism through which he

---

[1] A positivist is one who rejects what is not, at least in principle, verifiable in experience. An ontological proposition for Maritain is a statement about what is real that is not entirely verifiable in sense-experience even in principle.—Ed.

shapes himself as a human person—armed with knowledge, strength of judgment, and moral virtues—while at the same time conveying to him the spiritual heritage of the nation and the civilization in which he is involved, and preserving in this way the century-old achievements of generations. The utilitarian aspect of education—which enables the youth to get a job and make a living—must surely not be disregarded, for the children of man are not made for aristocratic leisure. But this practical aim is best provided by the general human capacities developed. And the ulterior specialized training which may be required must never imperil the essential aim of education.

Now in order to get a complete idea of the aim of education, it is necessary to take into closer consideration the human person and his deep natural aspirations.

The chief aspirations of a person are aspirations to freedom—I do not mean that freedom which is free will and which is a gift of nature in each of us, I mean that freedom which is spontaneity, expansion, or autonomy, and which we have to gain through constant effort and struggle. And what is the more profound and essential form of such a desire? It is the desire for inner and spiritual freedom. In this sense Greek philosophy, especially Aristotle, spoke of the independence which is granted to men by intellect and wisdom as the perfection of the human being. And the Gospel was to lift up human perfection to a higher level—a truly divine one—by stating that it consists of the perfection of love and, as St. Paul put it, of the freedom of those who are moved by the divine Spirit. . . . Thus the prime goal of education is the conquest of internal and spiritual freedom to be achieved by the individual person, or, in other words, his liberation through knowledge and wisdom, good will, and love.

. . . Truth—which does not depend on us but on *what is*—truth is not a set of ready-made formulas to be passively recorded, so as to have the mind closed and enclosed by them. Truth is an infinite realm—as infinite as being—whose wholeness transcends infinitely our powers of perception, and each fragment of which must be grasped through vital and purified internal activity. This conquest of being, this progressive attainment of new truths, or the progressive realization of the ever-growing and ever-renewed significance of truths already attained, opens and enlarges our mind and life, and really situates them in freedom and autonomy. And speaking of will and love rather than knowledge, no one is freer, or more independent, than the one who gives himself for a cause or a real being worthy of the gift.

Here we find ourselves confronted with the inappropriateness of the pragmatic overemphasis in education. . . . Many things are excellent in the emphasis on action and "praxis," for life consists of action.[2] But action and praxis aim at an object, a determining end without which they lose direction and vitality. And life exists, too, for an end which makes it worthy of being lived. Contemplation and self-perfection, in which human life aspires to flower forth, escape the purview of the pragmatic mind.

. . . It is because every human idea, to have a meaning, must attain in some measure (be it even in the symbols of a mathematical interpretation of phenomena), what things *are* or consist of unto themselves; it is because human thought is an instrument or rather a vital energy of knowledge or spiritual intuition (I don't mean "knowledge about," I mean "knowledge into"); it is because thinking begins, not only with difficulties but with *insights,* and ends up in insights which are made true by rational proving or experimental verifying, not by pragmatic sanction, that human thought is able to illumine experience, to realize desires which are human because they are rooted in the prime desire for unlimited good, and to dominate, control, and refashion the world. At the beginning of human action, insofar as it is human, there is truth, grasped or believed to be grasped for the sake of truth. Without trust in truth, there is no human effectiveness. Such is, to my mind, the chief criticism to be made of the pragmatic and instrumentalist theory of knowledge.[3] . . .

I have spoken of the aspiration of the human person to freedom, and, first of all, to inner and spiritual freedom. The second essential form of this desire is the desire for freedom externally manifested, and this freedom is linked to social life and lies at its very root. For society is "natural" to man in terms not only of animal or instinctive nature but of human nature, that is, of reason and freedom. If man is a naturally political animal, this is so in the sense that society, required by nature, is achieved through free consent, and because the human person demands the communications of social life

---

[2] Praxis = practice.—Ed.

[3] Instrumentalism is the view, held by Dewey, that thought is an instrument of action.—Ed.

through the openness and generosity proper to intelligence and love as well as through the needs of a human individual born naked and destitute. Thus it is that social life tends to emancipate man from the bondage of material nature. It subordinates the individual to the common good, but always in order that the common good flow back upon the individuals, and that they enjoy that freedom of expansion or independence which is insured by the economic guarantees of labor and ownership, political rights, civil virtues, and the cultivation of the mind.

As a result, it is obvious that man's education must be concerned with the social group and prepare him to play his part in it. Shaping man to lead a normal, useful and coöperative life in the community, or guiding the development of the human person in the social sphere, awakening and strengthening both his sense of freedom and his sense of obligation and responsibility, is an essential aim. But it is not the primary, it is the secondary essential aim. The ultimate end of education concerns the human person in his personal life and spiritual progress, not in his relationship to the social environment. . . . The essence of education does not consist in adapting a potential citizen to the conditions and interactions of social life, but first in *making a man,* and by this very fact in preparing a citizen. Not only is it nonsense to oppose education for the person and education for the commonwealth, but the latter supposes the former as a prerequisite, and in return the former is impossible without the latter, for one does not make a man except in the bosom of social ties where there is an awakening of civic understanding and civic virtues. . . .

To discuss the matter in a more specific manner, I should like to make the following observations: that conception which makes education itself a constantly renewed experiment, starting from the pupil's present purposes and developing in one way or another according to the success of his problem-solving activity with regard to these purposes and to new purposes arising from broadened experience in unforeseen directions, such a pragmatist conception has its own merits when it comes to the necessity of adapting educational methods to the natural interests of the pupil. But what are the standards for judging the purposes and values thus successively emerging in the pupil's mind? If the teacher himself has no general aim, nor final values to which all this process is related; if education itself is to grow "in whatever direction a novelly emerging future renders most feasible"; in other words, if the pragmatist theory requires a perpetual experimental reconstruction of the ends of the educator himself (and not only of the experience of the pupil), then it teaches educational recipes but gets away from any real art of education: for an education which does not have any goal of its own and tends only to growth itself without "end beyond further growth" is no more an art than an art of architecture which would not have any idea of what is to be built, and would only tend to the growth of the construction in whatever direction a new addition of materials is feasible. In nature itself, biological growth is nothing but a morphological process, or the progressive acquisition of a definite form. And finally the pragmatist theory can only subordinate and enslave education to the trends which may develop in collective life and society, for in the last analysis the aims newly arising in such a "reconstruction of ends" will only be determined by the precarious factors of the environment to be controlled and the values made at each moment predominant by given social conditions or tendencies or by the state.

The element of truth which must be preserved in the conception I have just discussed, is the fact that the final end of education—the fulfillment of man as a human person—is infinitely higher and broader than the aim of architectural art or even the aim of medical art, for it deals with our very freedom and spirit, whose boundless potentialities can be led to full human stature only by means of constant creative renewal. As a result, the vital spontaneity of the one to be educated plays a major part in the progress toward this final end, as well as the steady widening of the pupil's experience. . . .

If the nature and spirit of the child are the principal agent in education, then, obviously, the fundamental dispositions to be fostered in this principal agent are the very basis of the task of education. They are rooted in nature but they may be warped, and they need to be carefully cultivated. Without pretending to a complete enumeration, I should say that the fundamental dispositions are the five following ones:

First, the love of truth, which is the primary tendency of any intellectual nature. . . .

Second, the love of good and justice, and even the love of heroic feats, and this too is natural to the children of man.

Third, that disposition which might be called simplicity and openness with regard to existence. . . . I would describe this disposition as the attitude of a being who *exists* gladly, is unashamed of existing, stands upright in existence, and for whom to be and to accept the natural limitations of existence are matters of equally simple assent. . . .

The fourth fundamental disposition concerns the sense of a job well done, for next to the attitude toward existence there is nothing more basic in man's psychic life than the attitude toward work. I do not mean by this the habit of being hard working. . . . I am speaking of something deeper and more human, a respect for the job to be done, a feeling of faithfulness and responsibility regarding it. . . . I am convinced that when this fundamental disposition, which is the first natural move toward self-discipline, this probity in regard to work is marred, an essential basis of human morality is lacking.

The fifth fundamental disposition is the sense of coöperation, which is as natural in us, and as thwarted too, as the tendency to social and political life.

RICHARD S. PETERS

Must an Educator Have an Aim?

Richard S. Peters (1919–   ) is one of the post World War II analytical philosophers who belong to "the revolution in philosophy" which stems from G. E. Moore and Ludwig Wittgenstein and now largely dominates British philosophy (and to a much lesser extent our own). Unlike most such philosophers, he has written mainly on psychology and political theory, having an unusual background in both fields. He came thus to lecture and write on education, and is now Professor of the Philosophy of Education, University of London Institute of Education.

Many in recent times have blamed philosophers for neglecting their traditional task in relation to education. For, in the old days, it is argued, philosophers explained what the good life and the good society were; and this provided aims for educationists. But nowadays, as Sir Richard Livingstone put it, we are lacking in a knowledge of the 'science of good and evil'. I think that most modern philosophers would claim that, in this respect, they had advisedly neglected their traditional task, for the very good reason that they have become clearer about what their task as philosophers is. The so-called 'revolution in philosophy' of the twentieth century has been largely a matter of becoming clearer about what philosophy is and is not. And one of the conclusions that has emerged is that it is not a sort of super-science of good and evil.

However, this newly found modesty about providing blueprints for the good life does not altogether either excuse or explain the neglect by modern philosophers of philosophical problems connected with education. I do not think that this neglect springs from the conviction that there *are* no such philosophical problems. Rather it is because philosophers have been so concerned with their 'revolution' that they have concentrated more on the central problems of philosophy—those connected with knowledge and belief, appearance and reality, free-will and determinism, mind and body, space and time. Peripheral problems connected with concepts like 'education',

From Richard S. Peters, *Authority, Responsibility and Education* (2d ed.; London: George Allen & Unwin Ltd., 1963), pp. 83–95. Used by permission of Allen & Unwin, and of the author, with slight revisions by the author.

'authority', and 'character' have been crowded out, as Hobbes put it, 'no otherwise than the sun deprives the rest of the stars of light, not by hindering their action, but by obscuring and hiding them with his excess of brightness'. It is time that philosophers supplemented their sun-worship by a bit of star-gazing—but this, as I shall try to show, does not mean trying to return to the old task of constructing a horoscope of educational aims. . . .

Given that 'education' implies, first, some commendable state of mind and, secondly, some experience that is thought to lead up to or to contribute to it, and given also that people are usually deliberately put in the way of such experiences, it is only too easy to think of the whole business in terms of models like that of building a bridge or going on a journey. The commendable state of mind is thought of as an end to be aimed at, and the experiences which lead up to it are regarded as means to its attainment. For this model of adopting means to premeditated ends is one that haunts all our thinking about the promotion of what is valuable. In the educational sphere we therefore tend to look round for the equivalent of bridges to be built or ports to be steered to. Hence the complaints of lack of direction when obvious candidates do not appear to fill the bill.

It is my conviction that this model misleads us in the sphere of education. We have got the wrong picture of the way in which values must enter into education and this is what occasions the disillusioned muttering about the absence of agreed aims. But to bring out how we are misled we must look at the contexts where the means-end model *is* appropriate. There is, first of all, that of plans and purposes where we do things in order to put ourselves in the way of other things. We get on a bus in order to get to work; we fill up a form in order to get some spectacles. Our life is not just doing one thing after another; we impose plans and schedules on what we do by treating some as instrumental to others. Some of these we regard as more commendable than others, and what we call our scale of values bears witness to such choices. The second means-end context is that of making or producing things. We mix the flour in order to make a cake or weld steel in order to make a bridge. We speak of the end-product in a factory and of the means of production in an economic system.

In both these contexts we might well ask a person what he was aiming at, what his objective was. But in both cases the answer would usually be in terms of something pretty concrete. He might say something like 'getting a better job' or 'marrying the girl' in the first context; or something like 'producing a soundless aeroplane' in the second. Similarly if a teacher was asked what he was aiming at, he might state a limited objective like 'getting at least six children through the eleven-plus'. But he might, as it were, lift his eyes a bit from the scene of battle and commit himself to one of the more general aims of education—elusive things like 'the self-realization of the individual', 'character', 'wisdom', or 'citizenship'. But here the trouble starts; for going to school is not *a means* to these in the way in which getting on a bus is a means to getting to work; and they are not made or produced out of the material of the mind in the way in which a penny is produced out of copper. These very general aims are neither goals nor are they end-products. Like 'happiness' they are high-sounding ways of talking about doing some things rather than others and doing them in a certain manner. From an ethical point of view it is crucial to examine the concrete style and content of the activities falling under such generalized aims, as well as the interpersonal rules which they involve.

It might be objected that education is an art like medicine and that in medicine there is a commonly accepted end-product—physical health. Why should there not be a similar one for education—mental health, for instance? The answer is fairly obvious. Doctors deal mainly with the body and if they agree about what constitutes physical health it is because it can be defined in terms of physical criteria like temperature level and metabolism rate. Also there is little objection to manipulating and tinkering with the body in order to bring about the required result.

In the case of education, however, there are no agreed criteria for defining mental health; for either it designates something purely negative like the absence of unconscious conflicts, or, in so far as it is a positive concept, it has highly disputable personal and social preferences written into it. Also education is not, like medicine or psychiatry, a remedial business.[1] When we are concerned with the minds of men there are objections to bringing about positive results in certain sorts of ways. People make moral objections to pre-frontal leucotomy even as a remedial measure. How much more objection-

[1] For further discussion of this see R. S. Peters, "Mental Health as an Educational Aim," in *Aims of Education—The Philosophical Approach*, ed. T. Hollins (Manchester: University of Manchester Press, 1964).

able would it be to promote some more positive state of mind, like a love of peace, in all men by giving them drugs or operating on everyone at birth? Indeed, in my view, disputes between educationists, which take the form of disputes about aims, have largely been disputes about the desirability of a variety of principles involved in such procedures. Values are involved in education not so much as goals or end-products, but as principles implicit in different manners of proceeding or producing. . . .

To illustrate more clearly the distinction which I am drawing between 'aims' and 'principles of procedure', let me take a parallel from politics. A man who believes in equality, might, like Godwin, be lured by a positive picture of a society in which differences between people would be minimized. He might want to get rid of differences in wealth and rank, even to breed people in the attempt to iron out innate differences. He might even go so far as to advocate the abolition of institutions like the army or the Church in which some men were given opportunities of lording it over others. Another social reformer, however, might employ the principle of equality in a much more negative sense without any concrete picture to lure him on his journey. He might insist, merely, that whatever social changes were introduced, no one should be treated differently from anyone else unless a good reason could be produced to justify such unequal treatment. The Godwin type of man would rightly be regarded as pursuing equality as a very general aim; the more cautious Liberal would have no particular aim connected with equality. He would merely insist that whatever schemes were put forward must not be introduced in a way which would infringe his procedural principle.

I think that this is an illuminating parallel to the point I am trying to make about the aims of education. For, in my view, many disputes about the aims of education are disputes about principles of procedure rather than about 'aims' in the sense of objectives to be arrived at by taking appropriate means. The so-called 'aims' in part pick out the different valuations which are built into the different procedures like training, instruction, the use of authority, teaching by example and rational explanation, all of which fall under the general concept of 'education'.

Consider, for instance, the classic dispute about the aims of education which is so often connected with an argument about the derivation of the word 'education'.[2] There were those like Sir Percy Nunn who stressed the connection with *educere*—to lead out. For them the aim of education must therefore be the development or realization of individual potentialities. Others, like Sir John Adams, stressed the derivation from *educare*—to train, or mould according to some specification. They might be regarded as people who in fact believed in aims in a proper sense, in moulding boys into Christian gentlemen, for instance. The progressive who protests against this conception of education is not simply jibbing at the end-product of a Christian gentleman. He is also jibbing at the assimilation of education to an art where something is produced out of material. Rousseau, for instance, protested vociferously against treating children as little mannikins, as material to be poured into an adult mould. A child, he argued, should be treated with respect as a person. The progressive, therefore, like Dewey or Kilpatrick, presents another picture of the educational process. The child's interest must be awakened and he must be put into situations where the task rather than the man exerts the discipline. He will thus acquire habits and skills that are useful to him, and, by co-operating with others in common tasks, will develop respect for others and for himself. In the eyes of the progressive the use of authority as a principle of procedure is not only an inefficient way to pass on skills and information; it is also an immoral way to treat a child. It is made even worse in both respects by techniques like the use of reward and punishment.

So at the one end of the family tree generated by the concept of 'education' there are procedures involving the use of authority in which the voice and the cane are used to produce a desirable end-product. Education is here conceived in the image of fashioning an object in the arts. At the other end the importance of purposes and plans is stressed; but it is the purpose and planning of the child, not of the adult. As Rousseau put it: 'By attempting nothing in the beginning you would have produced an educational prodigy.'

But, as any educationist must know, if he reflects on the matter, these are only a limited selection of the procedures that are in fact employed. There is, for instance, the influence exerted by one person on another in some sort of apprenticeship system, when the

[2] For further discussion of the concept of "education" see R. S. Peters, "Education as Initiation," in *Philosophy of Education—A British View*, ed. R. Archambault (London: Routledge & Kegan Paul Ltd., 1964).

teacher guides rather than goads. We learn carpentry by doing it with someone who is a bit better at carpentry; we learn to think clearly by talking with someone who thinks a bit more clearly than we do. And this other person need not be a charismatic figure so beloved by the advocates of 'impressionism' in the public schools or Boy Scout movement. It may be a person who is not only skilled but who has the additional ability of being able to explain and give an account of what he is up to. Progressives often object to talk and chalk and confuse the use of the voice with one way in which it is used—the authoritative way. But most good teachers use their voices to excite and to explain, not simply to instruct, command, or drill.

My guess is that most of the important things in education are passed on in this manner—by example and explanation. An attitude, a skill, is caught: sensitivity, a critical mind, respect for people and facts develop where an articulate and intelligent exponent is on the job. Yet the model of means to ends is not remotely applicable to the transaction that is taking place. Values, of course, are involved in the transaction: if they were not it would not be called 'education.' Yet they are not end-products or terminating points of the process. They reside both in the skills and cultural traditions that are passed on and in the procedure for passing them on. . . .

There are all sorts of things that can be passed on that are valuable. Almost anything, as I started off by saying, can be regarded as being of educational value. And, to a large extent, those who favour one type of procedure rather than another choose examples that suit themselves and advocate the practice of things that can be passed on best in accordance with their favourite model. The man who advocates authority and drill is most at home with things like Latin and arithmetic where rules have simply to be learnt defining what is right or wrong and where, in the early stages at any rate, there is little scope for rational explanation or learning by experience. The progressive is most at home with things like art, drama, and environmental studies where projects can develop without too much artificiality. And the man who believes in rational instruction is usually inclined towards things like science, history, and geometry. . . .

. . . Of course, many of the things which we do can be regarded as ways of implementing concrete and limited objectives. But this picture of the pursuit of aims is often exalted into grandiose talk about the purpose of life or the purpose of political activity. Self-realization, the greatest happiness of the greatest number, and the classless society act as lures to provide a distant destination for the great journey of life.

Such general aims are not just harmless extravagances due to the overworking of a limited model of means to ends, a sort of metaphysical whistle in the dark. For men will do terrible things to other men in order to implement aims like racial purity which are both idiotic and illusory. The crucial question to ask, when men wax enthusiastic on the subject of their aims, is what *procedures* are to be adopted in order to implement them. We then get down to moral brass tacks. Do they in fact favour the model of implementing aims taken from the arts and from technology? There are those who favour the maximum of authoritative regulation such as is necessary in an army; there are those who use other people and mould them for their own purposes; there are those who are determined to live according to rational principles and to extend the maximum of toleration to others who disagree with them; there are those whose preoccupation is the pursuit of private good for whom hell is the other fellow.

These differences of procedure are writ large in the family, in economic affairs, and in political life. In education they are accentuated because the impact of man upon man is more conscious and because people are put into positions of authority where there is great scope for adopting their favoured procedures. My point is that arguments about the aims of education reflect these basic differences in principles of procedure. The Puritan and the Catholic both thought they were promoting God's kingdom, but they thought it had to be promoted in a different manner. And the different manner made it quite a different kingdom.

Of course arguments about general aims do not reflect *only* differences in principles of procedure or disagreements about the relative importance of public needs and individual development. Equally important are valuations of content where the merits of, e.g. art as distinct from those of science or history are under discussion. But the real issues involved in such comparisons are obscured by talk about self-realization, life, happiness, and so on. For what sort of self is to be realized? What quality of life is worth perpetuating? Teachers surely care whether or not poetry rather than push-pin is perpetuated, to use a time-honoured example. The problem of justifying such 'higher' activities is one of the most difficult and persistent problems in ethics. But talk about self-realization and other such omnibus 'ends' does more than obscure it; it also encourages an *instrumental* way of looking at the problem of justification. For a nebulous end is invented which such activities are supposed to lead up to, because it is erroneously assumed that education must be justified by reference to an end which is extrinsic to it. The truth is much more that there is a quality of life embedded in the activities which constitute education, and that 'self-realization' can be explicated only by reference to such activities. Thus, if by 'life' is meant what goes on outside schools and universities, there is an important sense in which 'life' must be for the sake of education, not education for life.

PART II

Education, Its Kinds, Methods, Programs, and Problems

J O H N   D E W E Y

Interest, Discipline, Method, and Subject Matter in Education

[INTEREST AND DISCIPLINE IN EDUCATION]

A person who is trained to consider his actions, to undertake them deliberately, is in so far forth disciplined. Add to this ability a power to endure in an intelligently chosen course in face of distraction, confusion, and difficulty, and you have the essence of discipline. Discipline means power at command; mastery of the resources available for carrying through the action undertaken. To know what one is to do and to move to do it promptly and by use of the requisite means is to be disciplined, whether we are thinking of an army or a mind. Discipline is positive. To cow the spirit, to subdue inclination, to compel obedience, to mortify the flesh, to make a subordinate perform an uncongenial task—these things are or are not disciplinary according as they do or do not tend to the development of power to recognize what one is about and to persistence in accomplishment.

It is hardly necessary to press the point that interest and discipline are connected, not opposed. . . . Interest measures—or rather is—the depth of the grip which the foreseen end has upon one in moving one to act for its realization.

Interest represents the moving force of objects—whether perceived or presented in imagination—in any experience having a purpose. In the concrete, the value of recognizing the dynamic place of interest in an educative development is that it leads to considering individual children in their specific capabilities, needs, and preferences. One who recognizes the importance of interest will not assume that all minds work in the same way because they happen to have the same teacher and textbook. Attitudes and methods of approach and response vary with the specific appeal the same material makes, this appeal itself varying with difference of natural aptitude, of past experience, of plan of life, and so on. . . .

Interest and discipline are correlative aspects of activity having an aim. Interest means that one is identified with the objects which define the activity and which furnish the means and obstacles to its realization. Any activity with an aim implies a distinction between an earlier incomplete phase and later completing phase; it implies also intermediate steps. To have an interest is to take things as entering into such a continuously developing situation, instead of taking them in isolation. The time difference between the given incomplete state of affairs and the desired fulfillment exacts effort in transformation; it demands continuity of attention and endurance. This attitude is what is practically meant by will. Discipline or development of power of continuous attention is its fruit.

The significance of this doctrine for the theory of education is twofold. On the one hand it protects us from the notion that mind and mental states are something complete in themselves, which then happen to be applied to some ready-made objects and topics so that knowledge results. It shows that mind and intelligent or purposeful engagement in a course of action into which things enter are identical. Hence to develop and train mind is to provide an environment which induces such activity. On the other side, it protects us from the notion that subject matter on its side is something isolated and independent. It shows that subject matter of learning is identical with all the objects, ideas, and principles which enter as resources or obstacles into the continuous intentional pursuit of a course of action. The developing course of action, whose end and conditions are perceived, is the unity which holds together what are often divided into an independent mind on one side and an independent world of objects and facts on the other. . . .

The problem of instruction is thus that of finding material which will engage a person in specific activities having an aim or purpose of moment or interest to him, and dealing with things not as gymnastic appliances but as conditions for the attainment of ends. The remedy for the evils attending the doctrine of formal discipline previously spoken of, is not to be found by substituting a doctrine of specialized disciplines, but by reforming the notion of mind and its training. Discovery of typical modes of activity, whether play or useful occupations, in which individuals are concerned, in whose outcome they recognize they have something at stake, and which cannot be carried through without reflection and use of judgment to select material of observation and recollection, is the remedy. In short, the root of the error long prevalent in the conception of training of mind consists in leaving out of account movements of things to future results in which an individual shares, and in the direction of which observation, imagination, and memory are enlisted. . . .

[EXPERIENCE, THINKING, AND EDUCATION]

So much for the general features of a reflective experience. They are (*i*) perplexity, confusion, doubt, due to the fact that one is implicated in an incomplete situation whose full character is not yet determined; (*ii*) a conjectural anticipation—a tentative interpretation of the given elements, attributing to them a tendency to effect certain consequences; (*iii*) a careful survey (examination, inspection, exploration, analysis) of all attainable consideration which will define and clarify the problem in hand; (*iv*) a consequent elaboration of the tentative hypothesis to make it more precise and more consistent, because squaring with a wider range of facts; (*v*) taking one's stand upon the projected hypothesis as a plan of action which is applied to the existing state of affairs: doing something overtly to bring about the anticipated result, and thereby testing the hypothesis. It is the extent and accuracy of steps three and four which mark off a distinctive reflective experience from one on the trial and error plane. They make *thinking* itself into an experience. Nevertheless, we never get wholly beyond the trial and error situation. Our most elaborate and rationally consistent thought has to be tried in the world and thereby tried out. And since it can never take into account all the connections, it can never cover with perfect accuracy all the consequences. Yet a thoughtful survey of conditions is so careful, and the guessing at results so controlled, that we have a right to mark off the reflective experience from the grosser trial and error forms of action.

In determining the place of thinking in experience we first noted that experience involves a connection of doing or trying with something which is undergone in consequence. A separation of the active doing phase from the passive undergoing phase destroys the vital meaning of an experience. Thinking is the accurate and deliberate instituting of connections between what is done and its consequences. It notes not only that they are connected, but the details of the connection. It makes connecting links explicit in the form of relationships. The stimulus to thinking is found when we wish to determine the significance of some act, performed or to be performed. Then we anticipate consequences. This implies that the situation as it stands is, either in fact or to us, incomplete and hence indeterminate. The projection of consequences means a proposed or tentative solution. To perfect this hypothesis, existing conditions have to be carefully scrutinized and the implications of the hypothesis developed—an operation called reasoning. Then the suggested solution—the idea or theory—has to be tested by acting upon it. If it brings about certain consequences, certain determinate changes, in the world, it is accepted as valid. Otherwise it is modified, and another trial made. Thinking includes all of these steps,—the sense of a problem, the observation of conditions, the formation and rational elaboration of a suggested conclusion, and the active experimental testing. While all thinking results in knowledge, ultimately the value of knowledge is subordinate to its use in thinking. For we live not in a settled and finished world, but in one which is going on, and where our main task is prospective, and where retrospect—and all knowledge as distinct from thought is retrospect—is of value in the solidity, security, and fertility it affords our dealings with the future.

The Essentials of Method. No one doubts, theoretically, the importance of fostering in school good habits of thinking. But apart from the fact that the acknowledgement is not so great in practice as in theory, there is not adequate theoretical recognition that all which the school can or need do for pupils, so far as their *minds* are concerned (that is, leaving out certain specialized muscular abilities), is to develop their ability to think. The parceling out of instruction among various ends such as acquisition of skill (in reading, spelling, writing, drawing, reciting); acquiring information (in history and geography), *and* training of thinking is a measure of the ineffective way in which we accomplish all three. Thinking which is not connected with increase of efficiency in action, and with learning more about ourselves and the world in which we live, has something the matter with it just as thought. . . . And skill obtained apart from thinking is not connected with any sense of the purposes for which it is to be used. It consequently leaves a man at the mercy of his routine habits and of the authoritative control of others, who know what they are about and who are not especially scrupulous as to their means of achievement. And information severed from thoughtful action is dead, a mind-crushing load. Since it simulates knowledge and thereby develops the poison of conceit, it is a most powerful obstacle to further growth in the grace of intelligence. The sole direct path to enduring improvement in the methods of instruction and learning consists in centering upon the conditions which exact, promote, and test thinking. Thinking *is* the method of intelligent learning, of learning that employs and rewards mind. We speak, legitimately enough, about the method of thinking, but the important thing to bear in mind about method is that thinking is method, the method of intelligent experience in the course which it takes.

I. The initial stage of that developing experience which is called thinking is *experience.* This remark may sound like a silly truism. It ought to be one; but unfortunately it is not. On the contrary, thinking is often regarded both in philosophic theory and in educational practice as something cut off from experience, and capable of being cultivated in isolation. In fact, the inherent limitations of experience are often urged as the sufficient ground for attention to thinking. Experience is then thought to be confined to the senses and appetites; to a mere material world, while thinking proceeds from a higher faculty (of reason), and is occupied with spiritual or at least literary things. So, oftentimes, a sharp distinction is made between pure mathematics as a peculiarly fit subject matter of thought (since it has nothing to do with physical existences) and applied mathematics, which has utilitarian but not mental value.

Speaking generally, the fundamental fallacy in methods of instruction lies in supposing that experience on the part of pupils may be assumed. What is here insisted upon is the necessity of an actual empirical situation as the initiating phase of thought. Experience is here taken as previously defined: trying to do something and having the thing perceptibly do something to one in return. The fallacy consists in supposing that we can begin with ready-made subject matter of arithmetic, or geography, or whatever, irrespective of some direct personal experience of a situation. Even the kindergarten and Montessori techniques are so anxious to get at intellectual distinctions, without "waste of time," that they tend to ignore —or reduce—the immediate crude handling of the familiar material of experience, and to introduce pupils at once to material which expresses the intellectual distinctions which adults have made. But the first stage of contact with any new material, at whatever age of maturity, must inevitably be of the trial and error sort. An individual must actually try, in play or work, to do something with material in carrying out his own impulsive activity, and then note the interaction of his energy and that of the material employed. This is what happens when a child at first begins to build with blocks, and it is equally what happens when a scientific man in his laboratory begins to experiment with unfamiliar objects.

Hence the first approach to any subject in school, if thought is to be aroused and not words acquired, should be as unscholastic as possible. To realize what an experience, or empirical situation, means, we have to call to mind the sort of situation that presents itself outside of school; the sort of occupations that interest and engage activity in ordinary life. And careful inspection of methods which are permanently successful in formal education, whether in arithmetic or learning to read, or studying geography, or learning physics or a foreign language, will reveal that they depend for their efficiency upon the fact that they go back to the type of the situation which causes reflection out of school in ordinary life. They give the pupils something to do, not something to learn; and the doing is of such a nature as to demand thinking, or the intentional noting of connections; learning naturally results.

That the situation should be of such a nature as to arouse thinking means of course that it should suggest something to do which is not either routine or capricious—something, in other words, presenting what is new (and hence uncertain or problematic) and yet sufficiently connected with existing habits to call out an effective response. An effective response means one which accomplishes a perceptible result, in distinction from a purely haphazard activity, where the consequences cannot be mentally connected with what is done. The most significant question which can be asked, accordingly, about any situation or experience proposed to induce learning is what quality of problem it involves.

At first thought, it might seem as if usual school methods measured well up to the standard here set. The giving of problems, the putting of questions, the assigning of tasks, the magnifying of difficulties, is a large part of school work. But it is indispensable to discriminate between genuine and simulated or mock problems. The following questions may aid in making such discrimination. (*a*) Is there anything but a problem? Does the question naturally suggest itself within some situation or personal experience? Or is it an aloof thing, a problem only for the purposes of conveying instruction in some school topic? Is it the sort of trying that would arouse observation and engage experimentation outside of school? (*b*) Is it the pupil's own problem, or is it the teacher's or textbook's problem, made a problem for the pupil only because he cannot get the required mark or be promoted or win the teacher's approval, unless he deals with it? Obviously, these two questions overlap. They are two ways of getting at the same point: Is the experience a personal thing of such a nature as inherently to stimulate and direct observation of the connections involved, and to lead to inference and its testing? Or is it imposed from without, and is the pupil's problem simply to meet the external requirement?

Such questions may give us pause in deciding upon the extent to which current practices are adapted to develop reflective habits. The physical equipment and arrangements of the average schoolroom are hostile to the existence of real situations of experience. What is there similar to the conditions of everyday life which will generate difficulties? Almost everything testifies to the great premium put upon listening, reading, and the reproduction of what is told and read. It is hardly possible to overstate the contrast between such conditions and the situations of active contact with things and persons in the home, on the playground, in fulfilling of ordinary responsibilities of life. Much of it is not even comparable with the questions which may arise in the mind of a boy or girl in conversing with others or in reading books outside of the school. No one has ever explained why children are so full of questions outside of the school (so that they pester grown-up persons if they get any encouragement), and the conspicuous absence of display of curiosity about the subject matter of school lessons. Reflection on this striking contrast will throw light upon the question of how far customary school conditions supply a context of experience in which problems naturally suggest themselves. No amount of improvement in the personal technique of the instructor will wholly remedy this state of things. There must be more actual material, more *stuff*, more appliances, and more opportunities for doing things, before the gap can be overcome. And where children are engaged in doing things and in discussing what arises in the course of their doing, it is found, even with comparatively indifferent modes of instruction, that children's inquiries are spontaneous and numerous, and the proposals of solution advanced, varied, and ingenious.

As a consequence of the absence of the materials and occupations which generate real problems, the pupil's problems are not his; or, rather, they are his *only as* a pupil, not as a human being. Hence the lamentable waste in carrying over such expertness as is achieved in dealing with them to the affairs of life beyond the schoolroom. A pupil has a problem, but it is the problem of meeting the peculiar requirements set by the teacher. His problem becomes that of finding out what the teacher wants, what will satisfy the teacher in recitation and examination and outward deportment. Relationship to subject matter is no longer direct. The occasions and material of thought are not found in the arithmetic or the history or geography itself, but in skillfully adapting that material to the teacher's requirements. The pupil studies, but unconsciously to himself the objects of his study are the conventions and standards of the school system and school authority, not the nominal "studies." The thinking thus evoked is artificially one-sided at the best. At its worst, the problem of the pupil is not how to meet the requirements of school life, but how to *seem* to meet them—or, how to come near enough to meeting them to slide along without an undue amount of friction. The type of judgment formed by these devices is not a desirable addition to character. If these statements give too highly colored a picture of usual school methods, the exaggeration may at least serve to illustrate the point: the need of active pursuits, involving the use of material to accomplish purposes, if there are to be situations which normally generate problems occasioning thoughtful inquiry.

II. There must be *data* at command to supply the considerations required in dealing with the specific difficulty which has presented itself. Teachers following a "developing" method sometimes tell children to think things out for themselves as if they could spin them out of their own heads. The material of thinking is not thoughts, but actions, facts, events, and the relations of things. In other words, to think effectively one must have had, or now have, experiences which will furnish him resources for coping with the difficulty at hand. A difficulty is an indispensable stimulus to thinking, but not all difficulties call out thinking. Sometimes they overwhelm and submerge and discourage. The perplexing situation must be sufficiently like situations which have already been dealt with so that pupils will have some control of the means of handling it. A large part of the art of instruction lies in making the difficulty of new problems large enough to challenge thought, and small enough so that, in addition to the confusion naturally attending the novel elements, there shall be luminous familiar spots from which helpful suggestions may spring.

In one sense, it is a matter of indifference by what psychological means the subject matter for reflection is provided. Memory, observation, reading, communication, are all avenues for supplying data. The relative proportion to be obtained from each is a matter of the specific features of the particular problem in hand. It is foolish to insist upon observation of objects presented to the senses if the student is so familiar with the objects that he could just as well recall the facts independently. It is possible to induce undue and crippling dependence upon sense-presentations. No one can carry around with him a museum of all the things whose properties will assist the conduct of thought. A well-trained mind is one that has a maximum of resources behind it, so to speak, and that is accustomed to go over its past experiences to see what they yield. On the other hand, a quality or relation of even a familiar object may previously have been passed over, and be just the fact that is helpful in dealing with the question. In this case direct observation is called for. The same principle applies to the use to be made of observation on one hand and of reading and "telling" on the other. Direct observation is natually more vivid and vital. But it has its limitations; and in any case it is a necessary part of education that one should acquire the ability to supplement the narrowness of his immediately personal experiences by utilizing the experiences of others. Excessive reliance upon others for data (whether got from reading or listening) is to be depreciated. Most objectionable of all is the probability that others, the book or the teacher, will supply solutions ready-made, instead of giving material that the student has to adapt and apply to the question in hand for himself.

There is no inconsistency in saying that in schools there is usually both too much and too little information supplied by others. The accumulation and acquisition of information for purposes of reproduction in recitation and examination is made too much of. "Knowledge," in the sense of information, means the working capital, the indispensable resources, of further inquiry; of finding out, or learning, more things. Frequently it is treated as an end itself, and then the goal becomes to heap it up and display it when called for. This static, cold-storage ideal of knowledge is inimical to educative development. It not only lets occasions for thinking go unused, but it swamps thinking. No one could construct a house on ground cluttered with miscellaneous junk. Pupils who have stored their "minds" with all kinds of material which they have never put to intellectual uses are sure to be hampered when they try to think. They have no practice in selecting what is appropriate, and no criterion to go by; everything is on the same dead static level. On the other hand, it is quite open to question whether, if information actually functioned in experience through use in application to the student's own purposes, there would not be need of more varied resources in books, pictures, and talks than are usually at command.

III. The correlate in thinking of facts, data, knowledge already acquired, is suggestions, inferences, conjectured meanings, suppositions, tentative explanations:—*ideas*, in short. Careful observation and recollection determine what is given, what is already there, and hence assured. They cannot furnish what is lacking. They define, clarify, and locate the question; they cannot supply its answer. Projection, invention, ingenuity, devising come in for that purpose. The data *arouse* suggestions, and only by reference to the specific data can we pass upon the appropriateness of the suggestions. But the suggestions run beyond what is, as yet, actually *given* in experience. They forecast possible results, things *to* do, not facts (things already done). Inference is always an invasion of the unknown, a leap from the known.

In this sense, a thought (what a thing suggests but is not as it is presented) is creative,—an incursion into the novel. It involves some inventiveness. What is suggested must, indeed, be familiar in *some* context; the novelty, the inventive devising, clings to the new light in which it is seen, the different use to which it is put. When Newton thought of his theory of gravitation, the creative aspect of his thought was not found in its materials. They were familiar; many of them commonplaces—sun, moon, planets, weight, distance, mass, square of numbers. These were not original ideas; they were established facts. His originality lay in the *use* to which these familiar acquaintances were put by introduction into an unfamiliar context. The same is true of every striking scientific discovery, every great invention, every admirable artistic production. Only silly folk identify creative originality with the extraordinary and fanciful; others recognize that its measure lies in putting everyday things to uses which had not occurred to others. The operation is novel, not the materials out of which it is constructed.

The educational conclusion which follows is that *all* thinking is original in a projection of considerations which have not been previously apprehended. The child of three who discovers what can be done with blocks, or of six who finds out what he can make by putting five cents and five cents together, is really a discoverer, even though everybody else in the world knows it. There is a genuine increment of experience; not another item mechanically added on, but enrichment by a new quality. The charm which the spontaneity of little children has for sympathetic observers is due to perception of this intellectual originality. The joy which children themselves experience is the joy of intellectual constructiveness—of creativeness, if the word may be used without misunderstanding.

The educational moral I am chiefly concerned to draw is not, however, that teachers would find their own work less of a grind and strain if school conditions favored learning in the sense of discovery and not in that of storing away what others pour into them; nor that it would be possible to give even children and youth the delights of personal intellectual productiveness—true and important as are these things. It is that no thought, no idea, can possibly be conveyed as an idea from one person to another. When it is told, it is, to the one to whom it is told, another given fact, not an idea. The communication may stimulate the other person to realize the question for himself and to think out a like idea, or it may smother his intellectual interest and suppress his dawning effort at thought. But what he *directly* gets cannot be an idea. Only by wrestling with the conditions of the problems at first hand, seeking and finding his own way out, does he think. When the parent or teacher has provided the conditions which stimulate thinking and has taken a sympathetic attitude toward the activities of the learner by entering into a common or conjoint experience, all has been done which a second party can do to instigate learning. The rest lies with the one directly concerned. If he cannot devise his own solution (not of course in isolation, but in correspondence with the teacher and other pupils) and find his own way out he will not learn, not even if he can recite some correct answer with one hundred per cent accuracy. We can and do supply ready-made "ideas" by the thousand; we do not usually take much pains to see that the one learning engages in significant situations where his own activities generate, support, and clinch ideas—that is, perceived meanings or connections. This does not mean that the teacher is to stand off and look on; the alternative to furnishing ready-made subject matter and listening to the accuracy with which it is reproduced is not quiescence, but participation, sharing, in an activity. In such shared activity, the teacher is a learner, and the learner is, without knowing it, a teacher—and upon the whole, the less consciousness there is, on either side, of either giving or receiving instruction, the better.

IV. Ideas, as we have seen, whether they be humble guesses or dignified theories, are anticipations of possible solutions. They are anticipations of some continuity or connection of an activity and a consequence which has not as yet shown itself. They are therefore tested by the operation of acting upon them. They are to guide and organize further observations, recollections, and experiments. They are intermediate in learning, not final. All educational reformers, as we have had occasion to remark, are given to attacking the passivity of traditional education. They have opposed pouring in from without, and absorbing like a sponge; they have attacked drilling in material as into hard and resisting rock. But it is not easy to secure conditions which will make the getting of an idea identical with having an experience which widens and makes more precise our contact with the environment. Activity, even self-activity, is too easily thought of as something merely mental, cooped up within the head, or finding expression only through the vocal organs.

While the need of application of ideas gained in study is acknowledged by all the more successful methods of instruction, the exercises in application are sometimes treated as devices for *fixing* what has already been learned and for getting greater practical skill in its manipulation. These results are genuine and not to be despised. But practice in applying what has been gained in study ought primarily to have an intellectual quality. As we have already seen, thoughts just as thoughts are incomplete. At best they are tentative; they are suggestions, indications. They are standpoints and methods for dealing with situations of experience. Till they are applied in these situations they lack full point and reality. Only application tests them, and only testing confers full meaning and a sense of their reality. Short of use made of them, they tend to segregate into a peculiar world of their own. It may be seriously questioned whether the philosophies . . . which isolate mind and set it over against the world did not have their origin in the fact that the reflective or theoretical class of men elaborated a large stock of ideas which social conditions did not allow them to act upon and test. Consequently men were thrown back into their own thoughts as ends in themselves.

However this may be, there can be no doubt that a peculiar artificiality attaches to much of what is learned in schools. It can hardly be said that many students consciously think of the subject matter as unreal; but it assuredly does not possess for them the kind of reality which the subject matter of their vital experiences possesses. They learn not to expect that sort of reality of it; they become habituated to treating it as having reality for the purposes of recitations, lessons, and examinations. That it should remain inert for the experiences of daily life is more or less a matter of course. The bad effects are twofold. Ordinary experience does not receive the enrichment which it should; it is not fertilized by school learning. And the attitudes which spring from getting used to and accepting half-understood and ill-digested material weaken vigor and efficiency of thought.

If we have dwelt especially on the negative side, it is for the sake of suggesting positive measures adapted to the effectual development of thought. Where schools are equipped with laboratories, shops, and gardens, where dramatizations, plays, and games are freely used, opportunities exist for reproducing situations of life, and for acquiring and applying information and ideas in the carrying forward of progressive experiences. Ideas are not segregated, they do not form an isolated island. They animate and enrich the ordinary course of life. Information is vitalized by its function; by the place it occupies in direction of action.

The phrase "opportunities exist" is used purposely. They may not be taken advantage of; it is possible to employ manual and constructive activities in a physical way, as means of getting just bodily skill; or they may be used almost exclusively for "utilitarian," *i.e.*, pecuniary, ends. But the disposition on the part of upholders of "cultural" education to assume that such activities are merely physical or professional in quality, is itself a product of the philosophies which isolate mind from direction of the course of experience and hence from action upon and with things. When the "mental" is regarded as a self-contained separate realm, a counterpart fate befalls bodily activity and movements. They are regarded as at the best mere external annexes to mind. They may be necessary for the satisfaction of bodily needs and the attainment of external decency and comfort, but they do not occupy a necessary place in mind nor enact an indispensable rôle in the completion of thought. Hence they have no place in a liberal education—*i.e.*, one which is concerned with the interests of intelligence. If they come in at all, it is as a concession to the material needs of the masses. That they should be allowed to invade the education of the élite is unspeakable. This conclusion follows irresistibly from the isolated conception of mind, but by the same logic it disappears when we perceive what mind really is—namely, the purposive and directive factor in the development of experience.

While it is desirable that all educational institutions should be equipped so as to give students an opportunity for acquiring and testing ideas and information in active pursuits typifying important social situations, it will, doubtless, be a long time before all of them are thus furnished. But this state of affairs does not afford instructors an excuse for folding their hands and persisting in methods which segregate school knowledge. Every recitation in every subject gives an opportunity for establishing cross connections between the subject matter of the lesson and the wider and more direct experiences of everyday life. Classroom instruction falls into three kinds. The least desirable treats each lesson as an independent whole. It does not put upon the student the responsibility of finding points of contact between it and other lessons in the same subject, or other subjects of study. Wiser teachers see to it that the student is systematically led to utilize his earlier lessons to help understand the present one, and also to use the present to throw additional light upon what has already been acquired. Results are better, but school subject matter is still isolated. Save by accident, out-of-school experience is left in its crude and comparatively irreflective state. It is not subject to the refining and expanding influence of the more accurate and comprehensive material of direct instruction. The latter is not motivated and impregnated with a sense of reality by being intermingled with the realities of everyday life. The best type of teaching bears in mind the desirability of affecting this interconnection. It puts the student in the habitual attitude of finding points of contact and mutual bearings.

Summary. Processes of instruction are unified in the degree in which they center in the production of good habits of thinking. While we may speak, without error, of the method of thought, the important thing is that thinking is the method of an educative experience. The essentials of method are therefore identical with the essentials of reflection. They are first that the pupil have a genuine situation of experience—that there be a continuous activity in which he is interested for its own sake; secondly, that a genuine problem develop within this situation as a stimulus to thought; third, that he possess the information and make the observations needed to deal with it; fourth, that suggested solutions occur to him which he shall be responsible for developing in an orderly way; fifth, that he have opportunity and occasion to test his ideas by application, to make their meaning clear and to discover for himself their validity.

[EDUCATIONAL VALUES AND THE CURRICULUM]

In one of its meanings, appreciation is opposed to depreciation. It denotes an enlarged, an *intensified* prizing, not merely a prizing, much less—like depreciation—a lowered and degraded prizing. This enhancement of the qualities which make any ordinary experience appealing, appropriable—capable of full assimilation—and enjoyable, constitutes the prime function of literature, music, drawing, painting, etc., in education. They are not exclusive agencies of appreciation in the most general sense of that word; but they are the chief agencies of an intensified, enhanced appreciation. As such, they are not only intrinsically and directly enjoyable, but they serve a purpose beyond themselves. They have the office, in increased degree, of all appreciation in fixing taste, in forming standards for the worth of later experiences. They arouse discontent with conditions which fall below their measure; they create a demand for surroundings coming up to their own level. They reveal a depth and range of meaning in experiences which otherwise might be mediocre and trivial. They supply, that is, organs of vision. Moreover, in their fullness they represent the concentration and consummation of elements of good which are otherwise scattered and incomplete. They select and focus the elements of enjoyable worth which make any experience directly enjoyable. They are not luxuries of education, but emphatic expressions of that which makes any education worth while. . . .

We cannot establish a hierarchy of values among studies. It is futile to attempt to arrange them in an order, beginning with one having least worth and going on to that of maximum value. In so far as any study has a unique or irreplaceable function of life, its worth is intrinsic or incomparable. Since education is not a means to living, but is identical with the operation of living a life which is fruitful and inherently significant, the only ultimate value which can be set up is just the process of living itself. And this is not an end to which studies and activities are subordinate means; it is the whole of which they are ingredients. And what has been said about appreciation means that every study in one of its aspects ought to have just such ultimate significance. It is true of arithmetic as it is of poetry that in some place and at some time it ought to be a good to be appreciated on its own account—just as an enjoyable experience, in short. If it is not, then when the time and place come for it to be used as a means or instrumentality, it will be in just that much handicapped. Never having been realized or appreciated for itself, one will miss something of its capacity as a resource for other ends.

It equally follows that when we compare studies as to their values, that is, treat them as means to something beyond themselves, that which controls their proper valuation is found in the specific situation in which they are to be used. The way to enable a student to apprehend the instrumental value of arithmetic is not to lecture him upon the benefit it will be to him in some remote and uncertain future, but to let him discover that success in something he is interested in doing depends upon ability to use number.

It also follows that the attempt to distribute distinct sorts of value among different studies is a misguided one, in spite of the amount of time recently devoted to the undertaking. Science for example may have *any* kind of value, depending upon the situation into which it enters as a means. To some the value of science may be military; it may be an instrument in strengthening means of offense or defense; it may be technological, a tool for engineering; or it may be commercial—an aid in the successful conduct of business; under other conditions, its worth may be philanthropic—the service it renders in relieving human suffering; or again it may be quite conventional—of value in establishing one's social status as an "educated" person. As matter of fact, science serves all these purposes, and it would be an arbitrary task to try to fix upon one of them as its "real" end. All that we can be sure of educationally is that science should be taught so as to be an end in itself in the lives of students—something worth while on account of its own unique intrinsic contribution to the experience of life. Primarily it must have "appreciation value." If we take something which seems to be at the opposite pole, like poetry, the same sort of statement applies. . . .

The same considerations apply to the value of a study or a topic of a study with reference to its motivating force. Those responsible for planning and teaching the course of study should have grounds for thinking that the studies and topics included furnish both direct increments to the enriching of lives of the pupils and also materials which they can put to use in other concerns of direct interest. Since the curriculum is always getting loaded down with purely inherited traditional matter and with subjects which represent mainly the energy of some influential person or group of persons in behalf of something dear to them, it requires constant inspection, criticism, and revision to make sure it is accomplishing its purpose. Then there is always the probability that it represents the values of adults rather than those of children and youth, or those of pupils a generation ago rather than those of the present day. Hence a further need for a critical outlook and survey. But these considerations do not mean that for a subject to have motivating value to a pupil (whether intrinsic or instrumental) is the same thing as for him to be aware of the value, or to be able to tell what the study is good for.

In the first place, as long as any topic makes an immediate appeal, it is not necessary to ask what it is good for. This is a question which can be asked only about instrumental values. Some goods are not good *for* anything; they are just goods. Any other notion leads to an absurdity. For we cannot stop asking the question about an instrumental good, one whose value lies in its being good *for* something, unless there is at some point something intrinsically good, good for itself. To a hungry, healthy child, food is a good of the situation; we do not have to bring him to consciousness of the ends subserved by food in order to supply a motive to eat. The food in connection with his appetite *is* a motive. The same thing holds of mentally eager pupils with respect to many topics. Neither they nor the teacher could possibly foretell with any exactness the purposes learning is to accomplish in the future; nor as long as the eagerness continues is it advisable to try to specify particular goods which are to come of it. The proof of a good is found in the fact that the pupil responds; his response *is* use. His response to the material shows that the subject functions in his life. It is unsound to urge that, say, Latin has a value *per se* in the abstract, just as a study, as a sufficient justification for teaching it. But it is equally absurd to argue that unless teacher or pupil can point out some definite assignable future use to which it is to be put, it lacks justifying value. When pupils are genuinely concerned in learning Latin, that is of itself proof that it possesses value. The most which one is entitled to ask in such cases is whether in view of the shortness of time, there are not other things of intrinsic value which in addition have greater instrumental value.

This brings us to the matter of instrumental values—topics studied because of some end beyond themselves. If a child is ill and his appetite does not lead him to eat when food is presented, or if his appetite is perverted so that he prefers candy to meat and vegetables, conscious reference to results is indicated. He needs to be made conscious of consequences as a justification of the positive or negative value of certain objects. Or the state of things may be normal enough, and yet an individual not be moved by some matter because he does not grasp how his attainment of some intrinsic good depends upon active concern with what is presented. In such cases, it is obviously the part of wisdom to establish consciousness of connection. In general what is desirable is that a topic be presented in such a way that it either have an immediate value, and require no justification, or else be perceived to be a means of achieving something of intrinsic value. . . .

[EDUCATION AND MORALS]

Morals is often thought to be an affair with which ordinary knowledge has nothing to do. Moral knowledge is thought to be a thing apart, and conscience is thought of as something radically different from consciousness. This separation, if valid, is of especial significance for education. Moral education in school is practically hopeless when we set up the development of character as a supreme end, and at the same time treat the acquiring of knowledge and the development of understanding, which of necessity occupy the chief part of school time, as having nothing to do with character. On such a basis, moral education is inevitably reduced to some kind of catechetical instruction, or lessons about morals. Lessons "about morals" signify as matter of course lessons in what other people think about virtues and duties. It amounts to something only in the degree in which pupils happen to be already animated by a sympathetic and dignified regard for the sentiments of others. Without such a regard, it has no more influence on character than information about the mountains of Asia; with a servile regard, it increases dependence upon others, and throws upon those in authority the responsibility for conduct. As a matter of fact, direct instruction in morals has been effective only in social groups where it was a part of the authoritative control of the many by the few. Not the teaching as such but the reënforcement of it by the whole régime of which it was an incident made it effective. To attempt to get similar results from lessons about morals in a democratic society is to rely upon sentimental magic.

At the other end of the scale stands the Socratic-Platonic teaching which identifies knowledge and virtue—which holds that no man does evil knowingly but only because of ignorance of the good. This doctrine is commonly attacked on the ground that nothing is more common than for a man to know the good and yet do the bad: not knowledge, but habituation or practice, and motive are what is required. Aristotle, in fact, at once attacked the Platonic teaching on the ground that moral virtue is like an art, such as medicine; the experienced practitioner is better than a man who has theoretical knowledge but no practical experience of disease and remedies. The issue turns, however, upon what is meant by knowledge. Aristotle's objection ignored the gist of Plato's teaching to the effect that man could not attain a theoretical insight into the good except as he had passed through years of practical habituation and strenuous discipline. Knowledge of the good was not a thing to be got either from books or from others, but was achieved through a prolonged education. It was the final and culminating grace of a mature experience of life. Irrespective of Plato's position, it is easy to perceive that the term knowledge is used to denote things as far apart as intimate and vital personal realization,—a conviction gained and tested in experience,—and a second-handed, largely symbolic, recognition that persons in general believe so and so—a devitalized remote information. That the latter does not guarantee conduct, that it does not profoundly affect character, goes without saying. But if knowledge means something of the same sort as our conviction gained by trying and testing that sugar is sweet and quinine bitter, the case stands otherwise. Every time a man sits on a chair rather than on a stove, carries an umbrella when it rains, consults a doctor when ill—or in short performs any of the thousand acts which make up his daily life, he proves that knowledge of a certain kind finds direct issue in conduct. There is every reason to suppose that the same sort of knowledge of good has a like expression; in fact "good" is an empty term unless it includes the satisfactions experienced in such situations as those mentioned. Knowledge that other persons are supposed to know something might lead one to act so as to win the approbation others attach to certain actions, or at least so as to give others the impression that one agrees with them; there is no reason why it should lead to personal initiative and loyalty in behalf of the beliefs attributed to them.

It is not necessary, accordingly, to dispute about the proper meaning of the term knowledge. It is enough for educational purposes to note the different qualities covered by the one name, to realize that it is knowledge gained at first hand through the exigencies of experience which affects conduct in significant ways. If a pupil learns things from books simply in connection with school lessons and for the sake of reciting what he has learned when called upon, then knowledge will have effect upon *some* conduct—namely upon that of reproducing statements at the demand of others. There is nothing surprising that such "knowledge" should not have much influence in the life out of school. But this is not a reason for making a divorce between knowledge and conduct, but for holding in low esteem this kind of knowledge. The same thing may be said of knowledge which relates merely to an isolated and technical specialty; it modifies action but only in its own narrow line. In truth, the problem of moral education in the schools is one with the problem of securing knowledge—the knowledge connected with the system of impulses and habits. For the use to which any known fact is put depends upon its connections. The knowledge of dynamite of a safecracker may be identical in verbal form with that of a chemist; in fact, it is different, for it is knit into connection with different aims and habits, and thus has a different import.

Our prior discussion of subject-matter as proceeding from direct activity having an immediate aim, to the enlargement of meaning found in geography and history, and then to scientifically organized knowledge, was based upon the idea of maintaining a vital connection between knowledge and activity. What is learned and employed in an occupation having an aim and involving coöperation with others is moral knowledge, whether consciously so regarded or not. For it builds up a social interest and confers the intelligence needed to make that interest effective in practice. Just because the studies of the curriculum represent standard factors in social life, they are organs of initiation into social values. As mere school studies, their acquisition has only a technical worth. Acquired under conditions where their social significance is realized, they feed moral interest and develop moral insight. Moreover, the qualities of mind discussed under the topic of method of learning are all of them intrinsically moral qualities. Open-mindedness, single-mindedness, sincerity, breadth of outlook, thoroughness, assumption of responsibility for developing the consequences of ideas which are accepted, are moral traits. The habit of identifying moral characteristics with external conformity to authoritative prescriptions may lead us to ignore the ethical value of these intellectual attitudes, but the same habit tends to reduce morals to a dead and machinelike routine. Consequently while such an attitude has moral results, the results are morally undesirable—above all in a democratic society where so much depends upon personal disposition.

All of the separations which we have been criticizing—and which the idea of education set forth in the previous chapters is designed to avoid—spring from taking morals too narrowly,—giving them, on one side, a sentimental goody-goody turn without reference to effective ability to do what is socially needed, and, on the other side, overemphasizing convention and tradition so as to limit morals to a list of definitely stated acts. As a matter of fact, morals are as broad as acts which concern our relationships with others. And potentially this includes all our acts, even though their social bearing may not be thought of at the time of performance. For every act, by the principle of habit, modifies disposition—it sets up a certain kind of inclination and desire. And it is impossible to tell when the habit thus strengthened may have a direct and perceptible influence on our association with others. Certain traits of character have such an obvious connection with our social relationships that we call them "moral" in an emphatic sense—truthfulness, honesty, chastity, amiability, etc. But this only means that they are, as compared with some other attitudes, central:—that they carry other attitudes with them. They are moral in an emphatic sense not because they are isolated and exclusive, but because they are so intimately connected with thousands of other attitudes which we do not explicitly recognize—which perhaps we have not even names for. To call them virtues in their isolation is like taking the skeleton for the living body. The bones are certainly important, but their importance lies in the fact that they support other organs of the body in such a way as to make them capable of integrated effective activity. And the same is true of the qualities of character which we specifically designate virtues. Morals concern nothing less than the whole character, and the whole character is identical with the man in all his concrete make-up and manifestations. To possess virtue does not signify to have cultivated a few nameable and exclusive traits; it means to be fully and adequately what one is capable of becoming through association with others in all the offices of life.

The moral and the social quality of conduct are, in the last analysis, identical with each other. It is then but to restate explicitly the import of our earlier chapters regarding the social function of education to say that the measure of the worth of the administration, curriculum, and methods of instruction of the school is the extent to which they are animated by a social spirit. And the great danger which threatens school work is the absence of conditions which make possible a permeating social spirit; this is the great enemy of effective moral training. For this spirit can be actively present only when certain conditions are met.

(i) In the first place, the school must itself be a community life in all which that implies. Social perceptions and interests can be developed only in a genuinely social medium—one where there is give and take in the building up of a common experience. Informational statements about things can be acquired in relative isolation by any one who previously has had enough intercourse with others to have learned language. But realization of the *meaning* of the linguistic signs is quite another matter. That involves a context of work and play in association with others. The plea which has been made for education through continued constructive activities in this book rests upon the fact they afford an opportunity for a social atmosphere. In place of a school set apart from life as a place for learning lessons, we have a miniature social group in which study and growth are incidents of present shared experience. Playgrounds, shops, workrooms, laboratories not only direct the natural active tendencies of youth, but they involve intercourse, communication, and coöperation,—all extending the perception of connections.

(*ii*) The learning in school should be continuous with that out of school. There should be a free interplay between the two. This is possible only when there are numerous points of contact between the social interests of the one and of the other. A school is conceivable in which there should be a spirit of companionship and shared activity, but where its social life would no more represent or typify that of the world beyond the school walls than that of a monastery. Social concern and understanding would be developed, but they would not be available outside; they would not carry over. The proverbial separation of town and gown, the cultivation of academic seclusion, operate in this direction. So does such adherence to the culture of the past as generates a reminiscent social spirit, for this makes an individual feel more at home in the life of other days than in his own. A professedly cultural education is peculiarly exposed to this danger. An idealized past becomes the refuge and solace of the spirit; present-day concerns are found sordid, and unworthy of attention. But as a rule, the absence of a social environment in connection with which learning is a need and a reward is the chief reason for the isolation of the school; and this isolation renders school knowledge inapplicable to life and so infertile in character.

how possible to "teach" morals

ALFRED NORTH WHITEHEAD

The Rhythmic Claims of Freedom and Discipline

The fading of ideals is sad evidence of the defeat of human endeavour. In the schools of antiquity philosophers aspired to impart wisdom, in modern colleges our humbler aim is to teach subjects. The drop from the divine wisdom, which was the goal of the ancients, to text-book knowledge of subjects, which is achieved by the moderns, marks an educational failure, sustained through the ages. I am not maintaining that in the practice of education the ancients were more successful than ourselves. . . . What I am anxious to impress on you is that though knowledge is one chief aim of intellectual education, there is another ingredient, vaguer but greater, and more dominating in its importance. The ancients called it "wisdom." You cannot be wise without some basis of knowledge; but you may easily acquire knowledge and remain bare of wisdom.

Now wisdom is the way in which knowledge is held. It concerns the handling of knowledge, its selection for the determination of relevant issues, its employment to add value to our immediate experience. This mastery of knowledge, which is wisdom, is the most intimate freedom obtainable. The ancients saw clearly—more clearly than we do—the necessity for dominating knowledge by wisdom. But, in the pursuit of wisdom in the region of practical education, they erred sadly. To put the matter simply, their popular practice assumed that wisdom could be imparted to the young by procuring philosophers to spout at them. Hence the crop of shady philosophers in the schools of the ancient world. The only avenue towards wisdom is by freedom in the presence of knowledge. But the only avenue towards knowledge is by discipline in the acquirement of ordered fact. Freedom and discipline are the two essentials of education. . . .

The antithesis in education between freedom and discipline is not so sharp as a logical analysis of the meanings of the terms might lead us to imagine. The pupil's mind is a growing organism. On the one hand, it is not a box to be ruthlessly packed with alien ideas: and, on the other hand, the ordered acquirement of knowledge is the natural food for a developing intelligence. Accordingly, it should be the aim of an ideally constructed education that the discipline should be the voluntary issue of free choice, and that the freedom should gain an enrichment of possibility as the issue of discipline. The two principles, freedom and discipline, are not antagonists, but should be so adjusted in the child's life that they correspond to a natural sway, to and fro, of the developing personality. It is this adaptation of freedom and discipline to the natural sway of development that I have elsewhere called The Rhythm of Education. I am convinced that much disappointing failure in the past has been due to neglect of attention to the importance of this rhythm. My main position is that the dominant note of education at its beginning and at its end is freedom, but that there is an intermediate stage of discipline with freedom in subordination: Furthermore, that there is not one unique threefold cycle of freedom, discipline, and freedom; but that all mental development is composed of such cycles, and of cycles of such cycles. Such a cycle is a unit cell, or brick; and the complete stage of growth is an organic structure of such cells. In analysing any one such cell, I call the first period of freedom the "stage of Romance," the intermediate period of discipline I call the "stage of Precision," and the final period of freedom is the "stage of Generalisation."

Let me now explain myself in more detail. There can be no mental development without interest. Interest is the *sine qua non* for attention and apprehension. You may endeavour to excite interest by means of birch rods, or you may coax it by the incitement of pleasurable activity. But without interest there will be no progress. Now the natural mode by which living organisms are excited towards suitable self-development is enjoyment. . . . Undoubtedly pain is one subordinate means of arousing an organism to action. But it only supervenes on the failure of pleasure. Joy is the normal healthy spur for the *élan vital*. I am not maintaining that we can safely abandon ourselves to the allurement of the greater immediate joys. What I do mean is that we should seek to arrange the development of character along a path of natural activity, in itself pleasurable. The subordinate stiffening of discipline must be directed to secure some long-time good; although an adequate object must not be too far below the horizon, if the necessary interest is to be retained.

The second preliminary point which I wish to make, is the unimportance—indeed the evil—of barren knowledge. The importance of knowledge lies in its use, in our active mastery of it—that is to say, it lies in wisdom. It is a convention to speak of mere knowledge, apart from wisdom, as of itself imparting a peculiar dignity to its possessor. I do not share in this reverence for knowledge as such. It all depends on who has the knowledge and what he does with it. That knowledge which adds greatness to character is knowledge so handled as to transform every phase of immediate experience. It is in respect to the activity of knowledge that an over-vigorous discipline in education is so harmful. The habit of active thought, with freshness, can only be generated by adequate freedom. Undiscriminating discipline defeats its own objects by dulling the mind. If you have much to do with the young as they emerge from school and from the university, you soon note the dulled minds of those whose education has consisted in the acquirement of inert knowledge. Also the deplorable tone of English society in respect to learning is a tribute to our educational failure. Furthermore, this over-haste to impart mere knowledge defeats itself. The human mind rejects knowledge imparted in this way. The craving for expansion, for activity, inherent in youth is disgusted by a dry imposition of disciplined knowledge. The discipline, when it comes, should satisfy a natural craving for the wisdom which adds value to bare experience.

But let us now examine more closely the rhythm of these natural cravings of the human intelligence. The first procedure of the mind in a new environment is a somewhat discursive activity amid a welter of ideas and experience. It is a process of discovery, a process of becoming used to curious thoughts, of shaping questions, of seeking for answers, of devising new experiences, of noticing what happens as the result of new ventures. This general process is both natural and of absorbing interest. We must often have noticed children between the ages of eight and thirteen absorbed in its ferment. It is dominated by wonder, and cursed be the dullard who destroys wonder. Now undoubtedly this stage of development requires help, and even discipline. The environment within which the mind is working must be carefully selected. It must, of course, be chosen to suit the child's stage of growth, and must be adapted to individual needs. In a sense it is an imposition from without; but in a deeper sense it answers to the call of life within the child. In the teacher's consciousness the child has been sent to his telescope to look at the stars, in the child's consciousness he has been given free access to the glory of the heavens. Unless, working somewhere, however obscurely, even in the dullest child, there is this transfiguration of imposed routine, the child's nature will refuse to assimilate the alien material. It must never be forgotten that education is not a process of packing articles in a trunk. Such a simile is entirely inapplicable. It is, of course, a process completely of its own peculiar genus. Its nearest analogue is the assimilation of food by a living organism; and we all know how necessary to health is palatable food under suitable conditions. . . .

This initial stage of romance requires guidance in another way. After all the child is the heir to long ages of civilisation, and it is absurd to let him wander in the intellectual maze of men in the Glacial Epoch. Accordingly, a certain pointing out of important acts, and of simplifying ideas, and of usual names, really strengthens the natural impetus of the pupil. In no part of education can you do without discipline or can you do without freedom; but in the stage of romance the emphasis must always be on freedom, to allow the child to see for itself and to act for itself. My point is that a block in the assimilation of ideas inevitably arises when a discipline of precision is imposed before a stage of romance has run its course in the growing mind. There is no comprehension apart from romance. It is my strong belief that the cause of so much failure in the past has been due to the lack of careful study of the due place of romance. Without the adventure of romance, at the best you get inert knowledge without initiative, and at the worst you get contempt of ideas—without knowledge.

But when this stage of romance has been properly guided another craving grows. The freshness of inexperience has worn off; there is general knowledge of the groundwork of fact and theory; and, above all, there has been plenty of independent browsing amid first-hand experiences, involving adventures of thought and of action. The enlightenment which comes from precise knowledge can now be understood. It corresponds to the obvious requirements of common sense, and deals with familiar material. Now is the time for pushing on, for knowing the subject exactly, and for retaining in the memory its salient features. This is the stage of precision. This stage is the sole stage of learning in the traditional scheme of education, either at school or university. You had to learn your subject, and there was nothing more to be said on the topic of education. The result of such an undue extension of a most necessary period of development was the production of a plentiful array of dunces, and of a few scholars whose natural interest had survived the car of Juggernaut. There is, indeed, always the temptation to teach pupils a little more of fact and of precise theory than at that stage they are fitted to assimilate. If only they could, it would be so useful. We—I am talking of schoolmasters and of university dons—are apt to forget that we are only subordinate elements in the education of a grown man; and that, in their own good time, in later life our pupils will learn for themselves. The phenomena of growth cannot be hurried beyond certain very narrow limits. But an unskilful practitioner can easily damage a sensitive organism. Yet, when all has been said in the way of caution, there is such a thing as pushing on, of getting to know the fundamental details and the main exact generalisations, and of acquiring an easy mastery of technique. There is no getting away from the fact that things have been found out, and that to be effective in the modern world you must have a store of definite acquirement of the best practice. To write poetry you must study metre; and to build bridges you must be learned in the strength of material. Even the Hebrew prophets had learned to write, probably in those days requiring no mean effort. The untutored art of genius is—in the words of the Prayer Book—a vain thing, fondly invented.

During the stage of precision, romance is the background. The stage is dominated by the inescapable fact that there are right ways and wrong ways, and definite truths to be known. But romance is not dead, and it is the art of teaching to foster it amidst definite application to appointed task. It must be fostered for one reason, because romance is after all a necessary ingredient of that balanced wisdom which is the goal to be attained. But there is another reason: The organism will not absorb the fruits of the task unless its powers of apprehension are kept fresh by romance. The real point is to discover in practice that exact balance between freedom and discipline which will give the greatest rate of progress over the things to be known. I do not believe that there is any abstract formula which will give information applicable to all subjects, to all types of pupils, or to each individual pupil; except indeed the formula of rhythmic sway which I have been insisting on, namely, that in the earlier stage the progress requires that the emphasis be laid on freedom, and that in the later middle stage the emphasis be laid on the definite acquirement of alloted tasks. I freely admit that if the stage of romance has been properly managed, the discipline of the second stage is much less apparent, that the children know how to go about their work, want to make a good job of it, and can be safely trusted with the details. Furthermore, I hold that the only discipline, important for its own sake, is self-discipline, and that this can only be acquired by a wide use of freedom. But yet—so many are the delicate points to be considered in education—it is necessary in life to have acquired the habit of cheerfully undertaking imposed tasks. The conditions can be satisfied if the tasks correspond to the natural cravings of the pupil at his stage of progress, if they keep his powers at full stretch, and if they attain an obviously sensible result, and if reasonable freedom is allowed in the mode of execution.

The difficulty of speaking about the way a skilful teacher will keep romance alive in his pupils arises from the fact that what takes a long time to describe, takes a short time to do. The beauty of a passage of Virgil may be rendered by insisting on beauty of verbal enunciation, taking no longer than prosy utterance. The emphasis on the beauty of a mathematical argument, in its marshalling of general considerations to unravel complex fact, is the speediest mode of procedure. The responsibility of the teacher at this stage is immense. To speak the truth, except in the rare case of genius in the teacher, I do not think that it is possible to take a whole class very far along the road of precision without some dulling of the interest. It is the unfortunate dilemma that initiative and training are both necessary, and that training is apt to kill initiative.

But this admission is not to condone a brutal ignorance of methods of mitigating this untoward fact. It is not a theoretical necessity, but arises because perfect tact is unattainable in the treatment of each individual case. In the past the methods employed assassinated interest; we are discussing how to reduce the evil to its smallest dimensions. I merely utter the warning that education is a difficult problem, to be solved by no one simple formula.

In this connexion there is, however, one practical consideration which is largely neglected. The territory of romantic interest is large, ill-defined, and not to be controlled by any explicit boundary. It depends on the chance flashes of insight. But the area of precise knowledge, as exacted in any general educational system, can be, and should be, definitely determined. If you make it too wide you will kill interest and defeat your own object: if you make it too narrow your pupils will lack effective grip. Surely, in every subject in each type of curriculum, the precise knowledge required should be determined after the most anxious inquiry. This does not now seem to be the case in any effective way. For example, in the classical studies of boys destined for a scientific career—a class of pupils in whom I am greatly interested—What is the Latin vocabulary which they ought definitely to know? Also what are the grammatical rules and constructions which they ought to have mastered? Why not determine these once and for all, and then bend every exercise to impress just these on the memory, and to understand their derivatives, both in Latin and also in French and English. Then, as to other constructions and words which occur in the reading of texts, supply full information in the easiest manner. A certain ruthless definiteness is essential in education. I am sure that one secret of a successful teacher is that he has formulated quite clearly in his mind what the pupil has got to know in precise fashion. He will then cease from half-hearted attempts to worry his pupils with memorising a lot of irrelevant stuff of inferior importance. The secret of success is pace, and the secret of pace is concentration. But, in respect to precise knowledge, the watchword is pace, pace, pace. Get your knowledge quickly, and then use it. If you can use it, you will retain it.

We have now come to the third stage of the rhythmic cycle, the stage of generalisation. There is here a reaction towards romance. Something definite is now known; aptitudes have been acquired; and general rules and laws are clearly apprehended both in their formulation and their detailed exemplification. The pupil now wants to use his new weapons. He is an effective individual, and it is effects that he wants to produce. He relapses into the discursive adventures of the romantic stage, with the advantage that his mind is now a disciplined regiment instead of a rabble. In this sense, education should begin in research and end in research. After all, the whole affair is merely a preparation for battling with the immediate experiences of life, a preparation by which to qualify each immediate moment with relevant ideas and appropriate actions. An education which does not begin by evoking initiative and end by encouraging it must be wrong. For its whole aim is the production of active wisdom.

In my own work at universities I have been much struck by the paralysis of thought induced in pupils by the aimless accumulation of precise knowledge, inert and unutilised. It should be the chief aim of a university professor to exhibit himself in his own true character—that is, as an ignorant man thinking, actively utilising this small share of knowledge. In a sense, knowledge shrinks as wisdom grows: for details are swallowed up in principles. The details of knowledge which are important will be picked up *ad hoc* in each avocation of life, but the habit of the active utilisation of well-understood principles is the final possession of wisdom. The stage of precision is the stage of growing into the apprehension of principles by the acquisition of a precise knowledge of details. The stage of generalisations is the stage of shedding details in favour of the active application of principles, the details retreating into subconscious habits. We don't go about explicitly retaining in our own minds that two and two make four, though once we had to learn it by heart. We trust to habit for our elementary arithmetic. But the essence of this stage is the emergence from the comparative passivity of being trained into the active freedom of application. Of course, during this stage, precise knowledge will grow, and more actively than ever before, because the mind has experienced the power of definiteness, and responds ,to the acquisition of general truth, and of richness of illustration. But the growth of knowledge becomes progressively unconscious, as being an incident derived from some active adventure of thought.

So much for the three stages of the rhythmic unit of development. In a general way the whole period of education is dominated by this threefold rhythm. Till the age of thirteen or fourteen there is the romantic stage, from fourteen to eighteen the stage of precision, and from eighteen to two and twenty the stage of generalisation. But these are only average characters, tinging the mode of development as a whole. I do not think that any pupil completes his stages simultaneously in all subjects. For example, I should plead that while language is initiating its stage of precision in the way of acquisition of vocabulary and of grammar, science should be in its full romantic stage. The romantic stage of language begins in infancy with the acquisition of speech, so that it passes early towards a stage of precision; while science is a late comer. Accordingly a precise inculcation of science at an early age wipes out initiative and interest, and destroys any chance of the topic having any richness of content in the child's apprehension. Thus, the romantic stage of science should persist for years after the precise study of language has commenced.

There are minor eddies, each in itself a threefold cycle, running its course in each day, in each week, and in each term. There is the general apprehension of some topic in its vague possibilities, the mastery of the relevant details, and finally the putting of the whole subject together in the light of the relevant knowledge. Unless the pupils are continually sustained by the evocation of interest, the acquirement of technique, and the excitement of success, they can never make progress, and will certainly lose heart. . . .

So far I have been discussing intellectual education, and my argument has been cramped on too narrow a basis. After all, our pupils are alive, and cannot be chopped into separate bits, like the pieces of a jig-saw puzzle. In the production of a mechanism the constructive energy lies outside it, and adds discrete parts to discrete parts. The case is far different for a living organism which grows by its own impulse towards self-development. This impulse can be stimulated and guided from outside the organism, and it can also be killed. But for all your stimulation and guidance the creative impulse towards growth comes from within, and is intensely characteristic of the individual. Education is the guidance of the individual towards a comprehension of the art of life; and by the art of life I mean the most complete achievement of varied activity expressing the potentialities of that living creature in the face of its actual environment. This completeness of achievement involves an artistic sense, subordinating the lower to the higher possibilities of the indivisible personality. Science, art, religion, morality, take their rise from this sense of values within the structure of being. Each individual embodies an adventure of existence. The art of life is the guidance of this adventure. The great religions of civilisation include among their original elements revolts against the inculcation of morals as a set of isolated prohibitions. Morality, in the petty negative sense of the term, is the deadly enemy of religion. Paul denounces the Law, and the Gospels are vehement against the Pharisees. Every outbreak of religion exhibits the same intensity of antagonism—an antagonism diminishing as religion fades. No part of education has more to gain from attention to the rhythmic law of growth than has moral and religious education. Whatever be the right way to formulate religious truths, it is death to religion to insist on a premature stage of precision. The vitality of religion is shown by the way in which the religious spirit has survived the ordeal of religious education.

The problem of religion in education is too large to be discussed at this stage of my address. I have referred to it to guard against the suspicion that the principles here advocated are to be conceived in a narrow sense. We are analysing the general law of rhythmic progress in the higher stages of life, embodying the initial awakening, the discipline, and the fruition on the higher plane. What I am now insisting is that the principle of progress is from within: the discovery is made by ourselves, the discipline is self-discipline, and the fruition is the outcome of our own initiative. The teacher has a double function. It is for him to elicit the enthusiasm by resonance from his own personality, and to create the environment of a larger knowledge and a firmer purpose. He is there to avoid the waste, which in the lower stages of existence is nature's way of evolution. The ultimate motive power, alike in science, in morality, and in religion, is the sense of value, the sense of importance. It takes the various forms of wonder, of curiosity, of reverence, or worship, of tumultuous desire for merging personality in something beyond itself. This sense of value imposes on life incredible labours, and apart from it life sinks back into the passivity of its lower types. The most penetrating exhibition of this force is the sense of beauty, the æsthetic sense of realised perfection. This thought leads me to ask, whether in our modern education we emphasise sufficiently the functions of art.

. . . You cannot, without loss, ignore in the life of the spirit so great a factor as art. Our æsthetic emotions provide us with vivid apprehensions of value. If you maim these, you weaken the force of the whole system of spiritual apprehensions. The claim for freedom in education carries with it the corollary that the development of the whole personality must be attended to. . . . History shows us that an efflorescence of art is the first activity of nations on the road to civilisation. Yet, in the face of this plain fact, we practically shut out art from the masses of the population. Can we wonder that such an education, evoking and defeating cravings, leads to failure and discontent? The stupidity of the whole procedure is, that art in simple popular forms is just what we can give to the nation without undue strain on our resources. . . . It would . . . require no very great effort to use our schools to produce a population with some love of music, some enjoyment of drama, and some joy in beauty of form and colour. We could also provide means for the satisfaction of these emotions in the general life of the population. . . .

Shakespeare wrote his plays for English people reared in the beauty of the country, amid the pageant of life as the Middle Ages merged into the Renaissance, and with a new world across the ocean to make vivid the call of romance. To-day we deal with herded town populations, reared in a scientific age. I have no doubt that unless we can meet the new age with new methods, to sustain for our populations the life of the spirit, sooner or later, amid some savage outbreak of defeated longings, the fate of Russia will be the fate of England. Historians will write as her epitaph that her fall issued from the spiritual blindness of her governing classes, from their dull materialism, and from their Pharisaic attachment to petty formulæ of statesmanship.

JACQUES MARITAIN

Intellectual and Moral Education

[THE ROLE OF THE TEACHER]

What is the kind of causality or dynamic action exerted by the teacher? Teaching is an art; the teacher is an artist. Is the teacher, then, like a sculptor, a powerful Michelangelo who belabors the marble or despotically imposes the form he has conceived on the passive clay? Such a conception was not infrequent in the education of old. It is a coarse and disastrous conception, contrary to the nature of things. For if the one who is being taught is not an angel, neither is he inanimate clay.

It is rather with the art of medicine that the art of education must be compared. Medicine deals with a living being that possesses inner vitality and the internal principle of health. The doctor exerts real causality in healing a sick man, yes, but in a very particular manner: by imitating the ways of nature herself in her operations, and by helping nature, by providing appropriate diet and remedies that nature herself uses, according to her own dynamism, toward a biological equilibrium. In other words, medicine is *ars cooperativa naturae*, an art of ministering, an art subservient to nature. And so is education. The implications of this are far-reaching indeed.

Ready-made knowledge does not, as Plato believed, exist in human souls. But the vital and active principle of knowledge does exist in each of us. The inner seeing power of intelligence, which naturally and from the very start perceives through sense-experience the primary notions on which all knowledge depends, is thereby able to proceed from what it already knows to what it does not yet know. An example of this is a Pascal discovering without any teacher and by virtue of his own ingenuity the first thirty-two propositions of the first book of Euclid. This inner vital principle the teacher must respect above all; his art consists in imitating the ways of the intellectual nature in its own operations. Thus the teacher has to offer to the mind either examples from experience or par-

From Jacques Maritain, *Education at the Crossroads* (New Haven, Conn.: Yale University Press, 1943). Used by permission of Yale University Press. [Taken from the paperbound edition (1960), pp. 22, 26–28, 30–33, 39–55, 55–57, 58–63, 94–96, *passim*.]

ticular statements which the pupil is able to judge by virtue of what he already knows and from which he will go on to discover broader horizons. The teacher has further to comfort the mind of the pupil by putting before his eyes the logical connections between ideas which the analytical or deductive power of the pupils' mind is perhaps not strong enough to establish by itself.

All this boils down to the fact that the mind's natural activity on the part of the learner and the intellectual guidance on the part of the teacher are both dynamic factors in education, but that the principal agent in education, the primary dynamic factor or propelling force, is the internal vital principle in the one to be educated; the educator or teacher is only the secondary—though a genuinely effective—dynamic factor and a ministerial agent. . . .

The freedom of the child is not the spontaneity of animal nature, moving right from the start along the fixed determinate paths of instinct (at least we usually think of animal instinct in this form, which is really too simplified, for animal instinct has a first period of progressive fixation). The freedom of the child is the spontaneity of a human and rational nature, and this largely *undetermined* spontaneity has its inner principle of final determination only in reason, which is not yet developed in the child.

The plastic and suggestible freedom of the child is harmed and led astray if it is not helped and guided. An education which consisted in making the child responsible for acquiring information about that of which he does not know he is ignorant, an education which only contemplated a blossoming forth of the child's instincts, and which rendered the teacher a tractable and useless attendant, is but a bankruptcy of education and of the responsibility of adults toward the youth. The right of the child to be educated requires that the educator shall have moral authority over him, and this authority is nothing else than the duty of the adult to the freedom of the youth. . . .

THE FUNDAMENTAL NORMS OF EDUCATION

. . . Assuredly, the primary rule is to foster those fundamental dispositions which enable the principal agent to grow in the life of the mind. It is clear, in this connection, that the task of the teacher is above all one of liberation. To liberate the good energies is the best way of repressing the bad ones, though repression is also needed, but only as a secondary means, . . . and even so it is useful only on condition that the repression of bad tendencies will always be bound up with enlightenment and encouragement. . . .

The second fundamental norm is to center attention on the inner depths of personality and its preconscious spiritual dynamism, in other words, to lay stress on inwardness and the internalization of the educational influence. . . .

The fathomless abyss of personal freedom and of the personal thirst and striving for knowing and seeing, grasping and expressing —I should call this the preconscious of the spirit in man. For reason does not consist only of its conscious logical tools and manifestations nor does the will consist only of its deliberate conscious determinations. Far beneath the apparent surface of explicit concepts and judgments, of words and expressed resolutions or movements of the will, are the sources of knowledge and poetry, of love and truly human desires, hidden in the spiritual darkness of the intimate vitality of the soul. Before being formed and expressed in concepts and judgments, intellectual knowledge is at first a beginning of insight, still unformulated, which proceeds from the impact of the illuminating activity of the intellect on the world of images and emotions and which is but a humble and trembling movement, yet invaluable, toward an intelligible content to be grasped. Parenthetically, it is with reference to this preconscious spiritual dynamism of human personality that keeping personal contact with the pupil is of such great import, not only as a better technique for making study more attractive and stimulating, but above all to give to that mysterious identity of the child's soul, which is unknown to himself, and which no techniques can reach, the comforting assurance of being in some way recognized by a human personal gaze, inexpressible either in concepts or words. . . .

Here we see that important and helpful changes might take place in our educational methods. Here it is not a question of techniques, nor of a training of the subconscious. It is rather a question of liberating the vital preconscious sources of the spirit's activity. Using Bergsonian language, I would say that in the education of the mind the emphasis should be shifted from that which is *pressure* (which, of course, remains somewhat necessary, but secondary) to that which awakens and frees the *aspirations* of spiritual nature in us.

Thus creative imagination, and the very life of the intellect, would not be sacrificed to cramming memorization or to conventional rule of skill in making use of concepts or words, or to the honest and conscientious but mechanical and hopeless cultivation of overspecialized fields of learning. . . .

What matters most in the life of reason is intellectual insight or intuition. There is no training or learning for that. Yet if the teacher keeps in view above all the inner center of vitality at work in the preconscious depths of the life of the intelligence, he may center the acquisition of knowledge and solid formation of the mind on the freeing of the child's and the youth's intuitive power. By what means? By moving forward along the paths of spontaneous interest and natural curiosity, by grounding the exercise of memory in intelligence, and primarily by giving courage, by listening a great deal, and by causing the youth to trust and give expression to those spontaneous poetic or noetic impulses of his own which seem to him fragile and bizarre, because they are not assured by any social sanction—and in fact any awkward gesture or rebuff or untimely advice on the part of the teacher can crush such timid sproutings and push them back into the shell of the unconsciousness. . . .

I come now to the third fundamental rule, which I shall try to express as follows: the whole work of education and teaching must tend to unify, not to spread out; it must strive to foster internal unity in man.

This means that from the very start, and, as far as possible, all through the years of youth, hands and mind should be at work together. This point has been made particularly clear by modern pedagogy as regards childhood. It is also valid for youth. The importance of manual work accompanying the education of the mind during the high school and college training is more and more recognized. There is no place closer to man than a workshop, and the intelligence of a man is not only in his head, but in his fingers too. Not only does manual work further psychological equilibrium, but it also furthers ingenuity and accuracy of the mind, and is the prime basis of artistic activity. . . .

Finally there is a fourth fundamental rule, which demands that teaching liberate intelligence instead of burdening it, in other words, that teaching result in the freeing of the mind through the mastery of reason over the things learned. . . .

. . . What is learned should never be passively or mechanically received, as dead information which weighs down and dulls the mind. It must rather be actively transformed by understanding into the very life of the mind, and thus strengthen the latter, as wood thrown into fire and transformed into flame makes the fire stronger. But a big mass of damp wood thrown into the fire only puts it out. Reason which receives knowledge in a servile manner does not really know and is only depressed by a knowledge which is not its own but that of others. On the contrary, reason which receives knowledge by assimilating it vitally, that is, in a free and liberating manner, really knows, and is exalted in its very activity by this knowledge which henceforth is its own. Then it is that reason really masters the things learned.

. . . Does the liberation of the mind mean that what essentially matters is not the possession of knowledge but only the development of the strength, skill, and accuracy of man's mental powers, whatever the thing to be learned may be? This question is of tremendous significance, and the wrong answer has probably gone a long way to water down contemporary education.

. . . The knowledge which is "of most worth"—I don't mean which has the most practical value, I mean which makes the mind penetrate into those things which are the richest in truth and intelligibility—such knowledge affords by itself the best mental training, for it is by grasping the object and having itself seized and vitalized by truth that the human mind gains both its strength and its freedom. It is not by the gymnastics of its faculties, it is by truth that it is set free, when truth is really known, that is, vitally assimilated by the insatiable activity which is rooted in the depths of self. The opposition between knowledge-value and training-value comes from an ignorance of what knowledge is, from the assumption that knowledge is a cramming of materials into a bag, and not the most vital action by means of which things are spiritualized in order to become one with the spirit. In the knowledge which is "of most worth," notably in the liberal arts, to give the upper hand to mental training, or to the mere dialectical disquisition of how great works are made or how great thoughts go on, to give such training the upper hand over beauty to be delighted in or the truth to be apprehended and assented to, would be to turn upside down the natural and vital tendency of the mind and drift toward dilettantism. . . .

. . . If we begin by denying that any subject matter is in itself and by reason of truth more important than another, then we deny in reality that any subject matter has any importance in itself, and everything vanishes into futility. . . .

. . . We are facing there a result of the fact that too often contemporary education has deemed it suitable to substitute training-value for knowledge-value—in other words, mental gymnastics for truth, and being in fine fettle, for wisdom. . . .

THE INNER STRUCTURE
OF THE CURRICULUM

. . . There are school subjects—those whose knowledge is "of most worth"—the main value of which is knowledge-value. And there are subjects—those whose knowledge is "of least worth"—the main value of which (I don't say the only value) is that of training. I should like to place the latter in the category of play—in broadening, of course, the sense of this word—and the former in the category of learning. Play has an essential part, though secondary, in school life; it possesses a value and worth of its own, being the activity of free expansion and a gleam of poetry in the very field of those energies which tend by nature toward utility. In the category of play thus broadly understood, I should like to see many things which are taught in elementary and secondary education—not only games, sports, and physical training, but first of all that handicraft work and dexterity in mechanics of which I spoke earlier, and, moreover, everything that the school can fancy to give training in, gardening, beekeeping, rustic lore, even cooking, jam-making, home economics, and so forth, and what is known as artistic training insofar as the "arts" involved are what is called in French *les arts d'agrément*, and in English, if I am not mistaken, "accomplishments." All of these things are dignified if they are dealt with as play activity, not with too much seriousness or too many frowns, but with some free and poetical cheerfulness. They lose educational meaning and make the school ever so slightly absurd if they are dealt with as an activity of learning, and put on the same level as genuine learning.

Above the category of play comes the category of learning, devoted to those matters whose main value is knowledge-value. Here too I think it would be best to trace a line of demarcation. In a first division we would place those matters the knowledge of which concerns the intellectual instruments and logical discipline required for the achievements of reason, as well as the treasure of factual and experiential information which must be gathered in memory. In a second division should be placed those matters the knowledge of which refers directly to the creative or perceptive intuition of the intellect and to that thirst for seeing of which we spoke previously.

In the first division I should like to place grammar, with a view to comparative grammar and philology, logic, and languages, on the other hand history, national history as well as the history of man and civilization and especially the history of the sciences, with connected subjects such as geography; all this I should call the field of the pre-liberal arts. And I should like to see the second division as the field of liberal arts, by recasting the old sevenfold listing of the Middle Ages according to a strictly educational outlook and to the modern progress of knowledge. Our *trivium* would concern the creative activity of the mind, and beauty to be perceived and delighted in. To begin with, it would comprise that *Eloquence* represented by Calliope, the first Muse and the mother of Orpheus, that is to say, the art of thought-expression or creative-expression which is the very art of making the mind actually able to set free and manifest its creative insight and making it really master of its power of expression—an art the neglect of which is so harmful to modern youth, who often lose their sense of the worthiness and accuracy of words, and become unable even to compose, when they enter upon practical life, a clear and articulate report on commercial or industrial matters. Then we would have, as the second of the liberal arts, *Literature and Poetry*, and as the third one, *Music and Fine Arts*.

Our *quadrivium* would concern the knowing and rational activity, the intuitive and judicative activity of the mind—truth to be perceived and assented to "according to the worth of evidence." It would comprise first *Mathematics,* second, *Physics and the Natural Sciences,* third, *Philosophy*—I mean not only psychology, but also the philosophy of nature, metaphysics, and the theory of knowledge —and fourth *Ethics and Political and Social Philosophy,* and connected studies.

[THE STAGES OF EDUCATION]

As to the principal stages in education, let us note that there are three great periods in education. I should like to designate them as the rudiments (or elementary education), the humanities (comprising both secondary and college education), and advanced studies (comprising graduate schools and higher specialized learning). And these periods correspond not only to three natural chronological periods in the growth of the youth but also to three naturally distinct and qualitatively determinate spheres of psychological development, and, accordingly, of knowledge.

The physical structure of the child is not that of the adult, shortened and abridged. The child is not a dwarf man. Nor is the adolescent. And this is much truer and much more crucial as regards the psychological than the physical structure of the youth. In the realm of physical training, of psychophysical conditioning, of animal and experimental psychology, contemporary education has understood more and more perfectly that a child of man is not just a diminutive man. It has not yet understood this in the spiritual realm of knowing: because, indeed, it is not interested in the psychology of spiritual activities. How, therefore, could it do anything but ignore that realm? The error is twofold. First we have forgotten that science and knowledge are not a self-sufficient set of notions, existing for their own sakes, abstracted and separate from man. Science and knowledge don't exist in books, they do exist in minds, they are vital and internal energies and must develop therefore according to the inner spiritual structure of the mind in which they have their being.

Secondly, we act as if the task of education were to infuse into the child or the adolescent, only abridging and concentrating it, the very science or knowledge of the adult—that is to say, of the philologist, the historian, the grammarian, the scientist, etc., the most specialized experts. So we try to cram young people with a chaos of summarized adult notions which have been either condensed, dogmatized, and textbookishly cut up or else made so easy that they are reduced to the vanishing point. As a result, we run the risk of producing either an instructed, bewildered intellectual dwarf, or an ignorant intellectual dwarf playing at dolls with our science. . . .

The knowledge to be given to youth *is not* the same knowledge as that of adults, it is an intrinsically and basically different knowledge, which is not knowledge in the state of science, such as that possessed by the mind of the adult, but the specific knowledge fitted to quicken and perfect the original world of thought of the child and the adolescent. Consequently I should like to emphasize that at each stage the knowledge must be of a sort fitted to the learners and conceived as reaching its perfection within their universe of thought during a distinct period of their development, instead of laying the foundations of a single sphere of knowledge which would grow in a continuous and uniform way until it became the science of the adult, where alone it would attain perfection.

The universe of a child is the universe of imagination—of an imagination which evolves little by little into reason. The knowledge which has to be given to the child is knowledge in a state of story, an imaginative grasp of the things and values of the world. The child's mentality may be compared in some ways with that of primitive man, and this mentality tends by itself toward magic, and whatever effort the teacher may make, his teaching always runs the risk of being caught and engulfed in a magic ocean. In his task of civilizing the child's mind, therefore, he must progressively tame the imagination to the rule of reason, whilst ever remembering that the proportionally tremendous work of the child's intellect, endeavoring to grasp the external world, is accomplished under the vital and perfectly normal rule of imagination.

I should like to add that beauty is the mental atmosphere and the inspiring power fitted to a child's education, and should be, so to speak, the continuous quickening and spiritualizing contrapuntal base of that education. Beauty makes intelligibility pass unawares through sense-awareness. It is by virtue of the allure of beautiful things and deeds and ideas that the child is to be led and awakened to intellectual and moral life. . . .

The universe of the adolescent is a transition state on the way to the universe of man. Judgment and intellectual strength are developing but are not yet really acquired. Such a mobile and anxious universe evolves under the rule of the natural impulses and tendencies of intelligence—and intelligence which is not yet matured and strengthened by those inner living energies, the sciences, arts, and wisdom, but which is sharp and fresh, eager to pass judgment on everything, and both trustful and exacting, and which craves intuitive sight. The knowledge which has to develop in the adolescent is knowledge appealing to the natural powers and gifts of the mind, knowledge as tending toward all things by the natural instinct of intelligence. The mental atmosphere for adolescence should be one of truth to be embraced. Truth is the inspiring force needed in the education of the youth—truth rather than erudition and self-consciousness—all-pervading truth rather than the objectively isolated truth at which each of the diverse sciences aims. Here we are confronted with a natural and instinctive impulse toward some all-embracing truth, which must be shaped little by little to critical reflection. . . . Common sense and the spontaneous pervasiveness of natural insight and reasoning constitute the dynamic unity of the adolescent's universe of thought, before wisdom may achieve in man a stabler unity. Just as imagination was the mental heaven of childhood, so now ascending reason, natural reason with its freshness, boldness, and first sparkling ambitions, is the mental heaven of adolescence; it is with reasoning that adolescence happens to be intoxicated. Here is a natural impulse to be turned to account by education, both by stimulating and by disciplining reason.

. . . If we seek to characterize the general objective of instruction at the stage of college education, we might say the objective is less the acquisition of science itself or art itself than the grasp of their *meaning* and the comprehension of the truth or beauty they yield. It is less a question of sharing in the very activity of the scientist or the poet than of nourishing oneself intellectually on the results of their achievement. Still less is it a question of developing one's own mental skill and taste in the fashion of the dilettante by gaining a superficial outlook on scientific or artistic procedures or the ways and means, the grammar, logic, methodology thereof. What I call the *meaning* of a science or art is contained in the specific truth or beauty it offers us. The objective of education is to see to it that the youth grasps this truth or beauty by the natural power and gifts of his mind and the natural intuitive energy of his reason backed up by his whole sensuous, imaginative, and emotional dynamism. In doing that a liberal education will cause his natural intelligence to follow in the footsteps of those intellectual virtues which are the eminent merit of the real scientist or artist. The practical condition for all that is to strive to penetrate as deeply as possible into the great achievements of the human mind rather than to tend toward material erudition and atomized memorization. So I should say that the youth is to learn and know music in order to understand the meaning of music rather than in order to become a composer. He must learn and know physics in order to understand the meaning of physics rather than to become a physicist. Thus college education can keep its necessary character of comprehensive universality and at the same time till and cultivate the whole mind, made available and alive, for the tasks of man.

[MORAL EDUCATION]

We believe that intelligence is in and by itself nobler than the will of man, for its activity is more immaterial and universal. But we believe also that, in regard to the things or the very objects on which this activity bears, it is better to will and love the good than simply to know it. Moreover it is through man's will, when it is good, not through his intelligence, be it ever so perfect, that man is made good and right. A similar intermingling of roles is to be found in education, taken in its broadest sense. The upbringing of the human being must lead both intelligence and will toward achievement, and the shaping of the will is throughout more important to man than the shaping of the intellect. Yet, whereas the educational system of schools and colleges succeeds as a rule in equipping man's intellect for knowledge, it seems to be missing its main achievement, the equipping of man's will. . . .

Teaching's domain is the domain of truth—I mean speculative as well as practical truth. The only dominating influence in the school and the college must be that of truth, and of the intelligible realities whose illuminating power obtains by its own virtue, not by virtue of the human authority of the master's say-so, the assent of an "open mind," intending to pronounce one way or another "according to the worth of evidence." No doubt the child's "open mind" is still unarmed, and unable to judge "according to the worth of evidence"; the child must believe his teacher. But from the very start the teacher must respect in the child the dignity of the mind, must appeal to the child's power of understanding, and conceive of his own effort as preparing a human mind to think for itself. The one who does not yet know must believe a master, but only in order to know, and maybe to reject at this very moment the opinions of the master; and he believes him provisionally, only because of the truth which the teacher is supposed to convey.

Thus it is chiefly through the instrumentality of intelligence and truth that the school and the college may affect the powers of desire, will, and love in the youth, and help him gain control of his tendential dynamism. Moral education plays an essential part in school and college education, and this part must be more and more emphasized.

But it is essentially and above all by way of knowledge and teaching that school education must perform this moral task, that is to say, not by exercising and giving rectitude to the will—nor by merely illuminating and giving rectitude to speculative reason—but by illuminating and giving rectitude to practical reason. The forgetting of this distinction between *will* and *practical reason* explains the above-mentioned failure of school pedagogy in its attempts to "educate the will."

Now as concerns the will itself, and the so-called "education of the will" or character-building (let us say, more accurately, with regard to the attainment of moral virtues and spiritual freedom), the specific task of school education amounts essentially to the two following points: first, the teacher must be solidly instructed in and deeply aware of the psychology of the child, less in order to form the latter's will and feelings than in order to avoid deforming or wounding them by pedagogical blunders to which unfortunately adults seem naturally inclined (here all of the modern psychological research may afford great help). Second, school and school life have to do, in an especially important manner, with what I would suggest calling "premoral" training, a point which deals not with morality strictly speaking, but with the preparation and first tilling of the soil thereof. Yet the main duty in the educational spheres of the school as well as of the state is not to shape the will and directly to develop moral virtues in the youth, but to enlighten and strengthen reason; so it is that an indirect influence is exerted on the will, by a sound equipment of knowledge and a sound development of the powers of thinking.

Thus the paradox of which I have spoken at such length comes to a solution: what is most important in the upbringing of man, that is, the uprightness of the will and the attainment of spiritual freedom, as well as the achievement of a sound relationship with society, is truly the main objective of education in its broadest sense. Concerning *direct* action on the will and the shaping of character, this objective chiefly depends on educational spheres other than school and college education—not to speak of the role which the extra-educational sphere plays in this matter. On the contrary, concerning *indirect* action on the will and the character, school and college education provides a basis and necessary preparation for the main objective in question by concentrating on knowledge and the intellect, not on the will and direct moral training, and by keeping sight, above all, of the development and uprightness of speculative and practical reason. School and college education has indeed its own world, which essentially consists of the dignity and achievements of knowledge and the intellect, that is, of the human being's root faculty. And of this world itself that knowledge which is wisdom is the ultimate goal. . . .

. . . What our present problem asks us to take into consideration is the large number of parents who are opposed to any religious education for their children. Here we are confronted anew with a peculiar task required today from the school system, and which is momentous. Additional emphasis should be brought to the teaching of natural morality. The normal way of giving this teaching, which is to have it embodied in the humanities, literature, and history . . . does not suffice in the face of the tremendous degradation of ethical reason which is observable today. For the moment the evil seems more apparent in our ideas than in our conduct, I mean in still civilized countries. Exhausted and bewildered by dint of false and dehumanized philosophy, reason confesses its impotence to justify any ethical standards. To such a disease of human intelligence and conscience, special remedies should be given, not only through the badly needed revival of religious faith but also through a revival of the moral power of reason. Accordingly, if teachers may be found whose reason is healthier than that of their students, special teaching should be provided, in schools and colleges, for the principles of natural morality.

Let us observe at this point that the field in which natural morality feels most at home, and least deficient, is the field of our temporal activities, or of political, civic, and social morality: because the virtues proper to this field are essentially natural ones, directed toward the good of civilization; whereas in the field of personal morality, the whole scope of the moral life cannot be comprehended by reason with regard to our real system of conduct in actual existence, without taking into account the supratemporal destiny of man So the teaching of natural morality will naturally tend to lay stress on what may be called the ethics of political life and of civilization. Which is all to the good (for here it enjoys its maximum strength and practical truth) provided that it resist the temptation of neglecting or disparaging personal morality, which is the root of all morality. Above all it should resist the temptation of warping and perverting all its work by making itself a tool of the state to shape youth according to the collective pattern supposedly needed by the pride, greed, or myths of the earthly community.

Now, since we are dealing with morality and moral teaching, we must not overlook the practical truth which is of the greatest moment in this regard: as to the actual uprightness of the will and human conduct, knowledge and sound teaching are necessary but are surely not enough. In order for us rightly to judge what to do in a particular case, our reason itself depends on the uprightness of our will, and on the decisive movement of our very freedom. The melancholy saying of Aristotle, contrasting with the Socratic doctrine that virtue is only knowledge, is to be recalled in this connection: "To know," he said, "does little, or even nothing, for virtue."

What does a great deal for virtue is love: because the basic hindrance to moral life is egoism, and the chief yearning of moral life liberation from oneself; and only love, being the gift of oneself, is able to remove this hindrance and to bring this yearning to fulfillment. But love itself is surrounded by our central egoism, and in perpetual danger of becoming entangled in and recaptured by it, whether this egoism makes the ones we love a prey to our devouring self-love or merges them in the ruthless self-love of the group, so as to exclude all other men from our love. Love does not regard ideas or abstractions or possibilities, love regards existing persons. God is the only person whom human love can fly to and settle in, so as to embrace also all other persons and be freed from egotistic self-love.

Love, human love as well as divine love, is not a matter of training or learning, for it is a gift; the love of God is a gift of nature and of grace: that is why it can be the first precept. How could we be commanded to put into action a power which we have not received or may not first receive? There are no human methods or techniques of getting or developing charity, any more than any other kind of love. There is nevertheless education in this matter: an education which is provided by trial and suffering, as well as by the human help and instruction of those whose moral authority is recognized by our conscience.

Here the educational sphere involved is first of all the family. Is not family love the primary pattern of any love uniting a community of men? Is not fraternal love the very name of that neighborly love which is but one with the love of God? No matter what deficiencies the family group may present in certain particular cases, no matter what trouble and disintegration the economic and social conditions of our day have brought to family life, the nature of things cannot be changed. And it is in the nature of things that the vitality and virtues of love develop first in the family.

RICHARD S. PETERS

Reason and Habit: The Paradox of Moral Education

The debate about whether and how virtue can be taught is a long-standing one in the history of ethics; but right at the very start, when Socrates and Protagoras were discussing the matter, Socrates characteristically made the point that the answers to the questions depended on what is meant by 'virtue.' Is it the 'correct opinion' and conventional behaviour of well-brought-up people?· Or is it conduct based on a grasp of fundamental principles? There is a corresponding difference in what is emphasized in moral education. On the one hand there is an emphasis on habit, tradition, and being properly brought up; on the other hand there is emphasis on intellectual training, and on the development of critical thought and choice.

It is not, however, necessarily the case either that these divergent accounts of morality are completely incompatible with each other or that there can be no rapprochement between their different emphases in matters of moral education. Indeed Aristotle attempted to combine both, but was led into a paradox about moral education which resulted from his attempt to stress the role both of reason and of habit. It is my intention in this paper both to combine these two emphases in moral education and to deal with the resulting paradox.

First of all it is necessary to follow Socrates' advice and attempt to get clearer about what morality is. This might be done by examining the use of 'moral' and its cognates in ordinary language. But it would be a long and detailed task for which there is little time in this lecture; for 'morality', like 'education', means very different things to different people. . . .

Behind, however, these vagaries of ordinary usage lies a distinctive form of discourse which has developed to answer distinctive forms of questions. These questions are concerned with what ought

From Richard S. Peters, "Reason and Habit: The Paradox of Moral Education," in *Moral Education in a Changing Society,* ed. W. R. Niblett (London: Faber & Faber Ltd., 1963), pp. 46–65. Used by permission of Faber & Faber, and of the author, with slight revisions by the author.

to be and with what ought to be done. This is a particular branch of what philosophers call practical discourse. Now practical discourse is not only concerned with answers to questions about what ought to be or what ought to be done. Commands, for instance, are also practical in that they are ways of getting people to do things by means of speech. But they differ from that form of practical discourse in which words like 'ought', 'good', 'right', and 'wrong' occur because there is no implied link with reasons. Saying, 'Shut the door,' or 'Shut up,' has a different social function from saying, 'You ought to shut the door,' or, 'Silence is a good thing.' Words like 'ought' and 'good' guide behaviour: they do not act as goads or stimuli for reactions. And they guide it with the suggestion that there are reasons for doing whatever is prescribed. . . .

Morality . . . is concerned with what there are reasons for doing or not doing, for bringing into or removing from existence. But this is only the start of the story; for what makes the reasons relevant ones? Supposing it is said that one ought not to slash people with razors, which is to suggest that there are reasons for not doing this. We inquire what the reasons are and are told that people bleed as a result and blood is red and that is why we should not do it. This would be a reason; but it would not appeal much to us as a good reason because it presupposes the principle that the redness in the world ought to be minimized, which most of us would regard as a somewhat bizarre principle. We would be more inclined to accept a reason like 'it hurts' because we regard the principle that *pain* ought to be minimized as more acceptable than the principle that *redness* ought to be minimized. . . .

It is manifest enough, however, that in respect of such a structure of rules we can be more or less prepared to justify, revise, or adapt them to changing circumstances. We can guide our lives by a host of rules which seem to us self-evident, or which might be backed up by the very general principle that we ought to do what others do or that we ought to do what X, who is in authority or an authority, says. Or we might try to live by a more rational and thought-out code. For men are creatures of habit and tradition in varying degrees. In a similar way we may be more or less intelligent in the application of rules to particular cases. This is the field of judgment, and whereas some men proceed with fine discrimination, others plod along boneheadedly by rules of thumb. Finally we can do what we should mechanically and with heavy hearts without caring overmuch for what we are doing, like reluctant housewives peeling potatoes. Or we can do what we should with more spontaneity because we genuinely care about that for the sake of which we are acting. In brief, the legislative, judicial, and executive aspects of our moral life can be more or less rationally, intelligently, and spontaneously conducted. . . .

I am a staunch supporter of a rationally held and intelligently applied moral code. Such a code seems peculiarly pertinent at the present time; for, as we have learnt in previous lectures, this is a time of rapid social change, of shifting standards both in regard to general social rules and in regard to activities which are thought to be worth-while, to which we are introduced in the curricula of schools and universities. . . .

. . . The peculiar pertinence of a rationally held moral code is that it can combine a degree of non-relativeness at one level with a degree of adaptability at another. Let me elucidate in a bit more detail both what I mean and where I stand.

To hold a rational code a man must subscribe to some higher-order principles which will enable him both to apply rules intelligently in the light of relevant differences in circumstances and to revise rules from time to time in the light of changes in circumstances and in empirical knowledge about the conditions and consequences of their application. The higher-order principles which, in my view, are capable of some sort of rational justification, are those of impartiality, truth-telling, liberty, and the consideration of interests. For these, I would argue, are presupposed by the very activity of giving reasons in practical discourse. These higher-order principles, though pretty formal in character, provide very general criteria of relevance for justifying particular rules and for making exceptions in particular cases.

Now just as it is possible for a scientist to stand firm on procedural principles like those of putting his theories up for public criticism, going by the evidence in deciding their truth, and not cooking evidence, and yet be willing to change the substantial content of such theories, so also is it possible for a man who holds a rational code to stick firmly to his principles at the procedural level —i.e. the principles of impartiality, liberty, truth-telling, and the consideration of interests, and yet to revise what he thinks about the substantial content of rules at a lower level—e.g. about smoking, gambling, or birth-control.

The criticism is often levelled against the advocates of a rationally held moral code that it would lead to moral anarchy. But why should it? For if the higher-order criterion of the impartial consideration of interests affected by rules is applied it will be seen that there are some rules which are so important for anyone living in a society that they could be regarded almost as definitions of a society. For a society is a collection of individuals united by the acceptance of certain rules, and though many of them relate to 'my station and its duties' (e.g. what ought to be done *qua* husband or *qua* teacher) there are also (leaving aside the law) a number of more general rules binding on anyone who is deemed to be a member of the same society—e.g. rules about the keeping of contracts, etc. . . . It would be difficult to conceive of any social, economic, or geographical changes which would lead one to think that such basic rules should be abrogated, though, of course, exceptions could be made to them under special circumstances. Such basic rules are to be contrasted with others which clearly do depend upon particular circumstances. Obviously, for instance, the rule that one should be sparing in the use of water is defensible only in times of drought. The fact that it is difficult to be sure to which category particular rules belong (e.g. about sexual behaviour) does not affect the general usefulness of the distinction. So in a rational code there would be procedural rules which could be regarded as presupposed by the very activity of giving reasons for rules; there would then be basic rules which would be those which could be justified under any conceivable social conditions; then there would be more relative rules which would depend, for their justifiability, on more contingent facts about particular social, economic, and geographical conditions. From the point of view of moral education it would be particularly important to pass on procedural rules and basic rules. . . . For in a time of rapid change it is important to pass on both a minimum equipment of basic rules together with procedural rules without which exceptions cannot be rationally made to basic rules or decisions taken about rules of a more relative status.

Moral education is usually associated with the transmission of such rules, but it is important to note that *all* education is necessarily a moral business; for, logically speaking, it must involve the transmission of what is worth-while. It would be a logical contradiction to say that a man had been educated but that he had changed in no way for the better. Worth-while development may take the form of initiation into worth-while activities as well as into desirable codes of conduct. Such good or worth-while activities were emphasized by the Ideal Utilitarians, such as Moore and Rashdall, who tended also to emphasize things like the pursuit of truth, the creation of beauty, the enjoyment of sensitive personal relationships, which defined the way of life of Keynes and other members of the Bloomsbury set at the beginning of this century. They rightly regarded the extension of such activities and of the outlook which goes with them as one of the main constituents in a civilized life. It would be a very difficult task and quite beyond the scope of this paper either to make a list of such activities or to show conclusively why the pursuit of them must be worth-while.[1] Nevertheless it is precisely these sorts of activities into which we strive to initiate children in schools. We do, presumably, aim at passing on poetry rather than push-pin. The promotion of such activities will be as important for those interested in the transmission of what is worth-while as the passing on of codes of conduct, with which moral education is usually equated.

Now within these worth-while activities it is generally possible to make the same sort of distinction between matters of procedure and matters of substance which I have made in the case of a rational code. Professor Oakeshott, in his fascinating essay entitled *The Teaching of Politics in a University*, makes a very similar distinction between what he calls the 'language' and 'literature' of a subject. To quote him: 'It is the distinction, for example, between the "language" of poetic imagination and a poem or novel; or between the "language" or manners of thinking of a scientist and a textbook of geology or what may be called the current state of our geological knowledge. . . . Science, for example, in a university, is not an encyclopaedia of information or the present state of our "physical" knowledge; it is a current activity, an explanatory manner of thinking and speaking being explored.' [2]

In such 'languages' are implicit various canons, or what I call rules of procedure, which permit the criticism, evaluation, and development of the 'literature'. The business of education generally,

---

[1] See A. P. Griffiths and R. S. Peters, *The Autonomy of Prudence*, Mind, April 1962.

[2] M. Oakeshott, *Rationalism in Politics and Other Essays*, Methuen, London, 1962, pp. 308, 311.

as well as moral education as it is usually conceived, consists largely in initiating people into the 'language' so that they can use it in an autonomous manner. This is done largely by introducing them to the 'literature'. And so we come to the paradox of moral education and of education in general.

What then is the paradox of moral education as I conceive it? It is this: given that it is desirable to develop people who conduct themselves rationally, intelligently and with a fair degree of spontaneity, the brute facts of child development reveal that at the most formative years of a child's development he is incapable of this form of life and impervious to the proper manner of passing it on. Let me spell out these facts in a little more detail.

Firstly, a fair amount of evidence has accumulated to demonstrate the decisive importance of early learning on later development. I refer here not simply to the evidence of Freudians, Kleinians, Bowlby and Harlow who have been concerned, roughly speaking, with the importance of early learning on the development of character and personality; I also refer to evidence produced by more physiologically minded psychologists such as Hebb.

Secondly, both the Freudian theory of the super-ego and Piaget's theory of the transcendental stage of the child's development converge to suggest that up to a certain age rules appear to a child as something external and unalterable, often sacred. Freud went further than Piaget in suggesting mechanisms, such as introjection and reaction-formation, by means of which these external sacrosanct rules come to be interiorized by the child and the standards adopted of that parent with whom identification takes place. It is not till later—well after the age of seven or eight—that what Piaget calls the autonomous stage develops when the notion dawns that rules can be otherwise, that they are conventions maintained out of mutual respect which can be altered if the co-operation of others can be obtained.

No doubt a similar point could be made also about a young child's attitude to the 'literature' of subjects such as geography, history and science. In so far as his minimal concepts of space, time, and causality enable him to grasp information handed on which belongs to the 'literature' of these disciplines, he will tend first of all to regard them as pronouncements from an oracle. Until he is gradually initiated into the 'language' of the subjects, by means of which he can begin to evaluate the literature, he will remain in the position of primitive people in respect of their attitude to the traditions of their tribe.

Thirdly, there is evidence to suggest—e.g. from Luria's experiments with manipulative tasks—that the giving of reasons has very little educative effect before a certain age. The explanations given by adults bite very little into the child's behaviour, though commands do have an effect at an earlier age.

Nevertheless, in spite of the fact that a rational code of behaviour and the 'language' of a variety of activities is beyond the grasp of young children, they can and must enter the palace of Reason through the courtyard of Habit and Tradition. This is the paradox of moral education which was first put so well by Aristotle in Book 2 of his *Nicomachean Ethics*.

The problem of moral education then, and indeed of education in general, is this: how can the necessary habits of behaviour and the deep-rooted assumptions of the 'literature' of various forms of good activities be acquired in a way which does not stultify the development of a rational code or the mastery of the 'language' of activities at a later stage?

I am assuming, by the way, like Aristotle, that children gradually acquire these desirable forms of life by some on-the-spot apprenticeship system. I am also assuming something about the factor which I previously picked out when I stressed the spontaneous enjoyment that goes with such a form of life. Spinoza put this in a very general way when he declared that, 'Blessedness is not the reward of right-living; it is the right living itself; nor should we rejoice in it because we restrain our desires, but, on the contrary, it is because we rejoice in it that we restrain them.'[3] In the jargon of modern psychology this is to say that a rational code and worth-while activities are intrinsically not extrinsically motivated.

Now education, at any rate at later levels, consists largely in initiating people into this form of life—in getting others on the inside of activities so that they practise them simply for the intrinsic satisfactions that they contain and for no end which is extrinsic to them. That is why one gets so impatient with the endless talk about the aims of education and the modern tendency to speak about education in the economic jargon of 'investment' and 'commodity'. No one, of course, would deny that many skills and much information

[3] Spinoza: *Ethics*, Part V., Prop. XLII.

have to be passed on to sustain and increase productivity in an industrial society; it is also the case that if money has to be raised from hard-headed business men or from an over-taxed and materialistically minded public, the instrumental aspects of what goes on in schools and universities may have to be stressed. But anyone who reflects must ask questions about the point of keeping the wheels of industry turning. And the answer is not simply that it is necessary for survival or 'living'—whatever that means. It is necessary for the maintenance and extension of a civilized life whose distinctive outlook and activities are those which are passed on in schools and universities. In such institutions there is no absolute distinction between teacher and learner. It is a matter of degree of skill, knowledge, insight and experience within a common form of life. So there is an important sense in which 'life', by which is usually meant that which goes on outside the class-room, is for the sake of education, not education for life. . . .

Now anyone who has managed to get on the inside of what is passed on in schools and universities, such as science, music, art, carpentry, literature, history, and athletics, will regard it as somehow ridiculous to be asked what the point of his activity is. The mastery of the 'language' carries with it its own delights, or 'intrinsic motivation', to use the jargon. But for a person on the *outside* it may be difficult to see what point there is in the activity in question. Hence the incredulity of the uninitiated when confronted with the rhapsodies of the mountain-climber, musician or golfer. *Children* are to a large extent in the position of such outsiders. The problem is to introduce them to a civilized outlook and activities in such a way that they can get on the inside of those for which they have aptitude.

The same sort of problem can be posed in the case of their attitude to rules of conduct. Is it the case that children have to be lured by irrelevant incentives or goaded by commands so that they acquire the basic habits of conduct and the 'literature' of the various activities without which they cannot emerge to the later stage? Is it the case that we have to use such irrelevant 'extrinsic' techniques to get children going so that eventually they can take over for themselves, without needing any longer such extrinsic incentives or goads? Or does the use of such extrinsic techniques militate against intelligent, spontaneous, and intrinsically directed behaviour later on?

It might be argued, for instance, that the various maturation levels bring with them the possibility of a variety of intrinsic motivations falling under concepts such as competence,[4] mastery, and curiosity. Then there is the ubiquitous role of love and trust; for psychoanalysts such as Bowlby suggest that the existence of a good relationship of love and trust between parent and child during the early years is a *necessary condition* for the formation of any enduring and consistent moral habits.[5] Whether love, the withdrawal of love, approval and disapproval, constitute extrinsic or intrinsic motivations in respect to the development of habits is too complicated a question to consider here. Nevertheless it may well be that the use of such intrinsic as distinct from extrinsic motivations may be crucial in determining the type of habits that are formed. For the formation of *some* types of habit may not necessarily militate against adaptability and spontaneous enjoyment. However, it is often thought that, because of the very nature of habits, dwelling in the courtyard of Habit incapacitates a man for life in the palace of Reason. I now propose to show both why this need not be the case and why people can be led to think that it must be the case. . . .

. . . The formation of sound moral habits in respect of, for instance, what I have called basic moral rules might well be a necessary condition of rational morality. It can, however, seem to be antagonistic to rational morality because of an interesting sort of conceptual confusion and because of the development, through a variety of causes, of specific types of habit. I will deal first with the conceptual issue and then proceed to the more empirical one.

What, then, do we mean by 'habits' and is there any necessary contradiction in stressing the importance of habit in moral matters while, at the same time, stressing the intelligent adaptability which is usually associated with reason, together with the spontaneous enjoyment associated with civilized activities? . . .

When we describe an action as a 'habit' we suggest, first of all, that the man has done this very thing before and that he will probably do it again. We are postulating a tendency to act in this way. 'Habit' also carries with it the suggestion not only of repetition but

[4] See, for instance, R. White: *Competence and the Psychosexual Stages of Development,* in Nebraska Symposium on Motivation 1960.

[5] See R. S. Peters: *Moral Education and the Psychology of Character,* Philosophy, January 1962.

also of the ability to carry out the action in question 'automatically'. A man can automatically stir his tea or puff his pipe while discussing the latest developments in Cuba. . . . The art of living consists to a large extent, in reducing most things that have to be done to habit; for then the mind is set free to pay attention to things that are interesting, novel, and worth-while. . . .

What are the implications of this analysis for the development of adaptability which is the hallmark of skilled and civilized activities? What we call a skill presupposes a number of component habits. A fielder at cricket, for instance, may be very skilful and show great intelligence in running a man out by throwing the ball to the bowler rather than to the wicket-keeper. But to do this he would have to bend down, pick the ball up, and contort his body with his eye partly on the ball and partly on the position of the batsmen. But unless these component actions were more or less habits he would not be able to concentrate on using them in the service of the higher strategy of the game. But—and this is the important point—all these component actions would have to be capable of being performed with a degree of plasticity to permit co-ordination in a wide variety of very different overall actions. The concept of 'action' is 'open-ended' in many dimensions. We could describe the man as moving his arm, as throwing the ball at the wicket, or throwing it at the bowler's end, or as running the batsman out, depending on the aspect under which the fielder conceived what he was doing. In what we call 'mechanical' actions a man will always conceive the movements as leading up in a stereotyped way to a narrowly conceived end. In intelligent actions the component actions are conceived of as variable and adaptable in the light of some more generally conceived end. The teachers who have taught me most about golf and about philosophy are those who have insisted on conveying an overall picture of the performance as a whole in which the particular moves have to be practised under the aspect of some wider conception, instead of concentrating either on drilling me in moves which are conceived in a very limited way or going simply for the overall picture without bothering about practising the component moves.

Now the type of habits which would count as moral habits *must* be exhibited in a wide range of actions in so far as actions are thought to be constituted by the sorts of movements of the body that are usually associated with skills. Consider, for instance, the range of such actions that can fall under the concept of theft or malice.

What makes an action a case of theft is that it must be conceived of as involving appropriating, without permission, something that belongs to someone else. A child, strictly speaking, cannot be guilty of theft, who has not developed the concept of himself as distinct from others, of property, of the granting of permission, etc. It takes a long time to develop such concepts. In the early years, therefore, parents may think that they are teaching their children not to steal, whereas in fact they are doing no such thing. They may be teaching the child something else, e.g. to inhibit actions of which authority figures disapprove, or to inhibit a narrowly conceived range of movements. At the toilet training stage, for instance, children may pick up very generalized and often unintelligent habits—e.g. punctilious conformity to rules, unwillingness to part with anything that is theirs. But this is not what the parents were trying to teach them. For the children probably lack the concepts which are necessary for understanding what the parents *think* that they are teaching them, namely the rule of cleanliness. To learn to act on rules forbidding theft, lying, breaking promises, etc., is necessarily an open-ended business requiring intelligence and a high degree of social sophistication. For the child has to learn to see that a vast range of very different actions and performances can fall under a highly abstract rule which makes them all examples of a type of action. If the child has really learnt to act on a rule it is difficult to see how he could have accomplished this without insight and intelligence. He might be drilled or forced to act in *accordance with* a rule; but that is quite different from learning to act *on* a rule.

So it seems as if the paradox of moral education is resolved. For there is no *necessary* contradiction between the use of intelligence and the formation of habits. How then does the antithesis between the two, which is frequently made, come about? Partly, I think, through the existence of certain explanatory expressions such as 'out of habit', and partly because of certain empirical facts about a special class of habits.

To take the point about explanatory expressions first. In explaining particular actions or courses of action we often use the phrase 'out of habit', 'through force of habit', or 'that is a matter of sheer habit'. This type of phrase does not simply suggest that what the man is doing is a habit in the sense that he has a tendency to do this sort of thing and that he can do it automatically. It also implies that in this case:

(i) The man has no reason for doing it which would render the action other than one conceived in a limited way. He could of course be raising his arm to attract someone's notice. He might indeed produce such a reason for doing it if asked. But to say that he raised his arm on this occasion 'out of habit' or through 'force of habit' is to deny that, on this occasion, such a reason which he might have, was *his* reason. Raising his arm *simpliciter*, we are saying, is just the sort of thing that he tends to do.

(ii) The clash with the idea of spontaneity, which is also often associated with 'habit', comes in also because to say that a man cleans his teeth or washes up 'out of habit' or 'through force of habit' is to exclude the possibility that there is any enjoyment in it for him, that he is doing it for pleasure, for what he sees in it as distinct from what he sees it leading on to. It is, in other words, to rule out intrinsic motivation. It is to explain what he does, roughly speaking, in terms of the law of exercise, and to rule out any variant of the law of effect. . . .

Given, then, that the explanation 'out of habit' or 'from force of habit' rules out the possibility of a further extrinsic end by reference to which an action could be deemed to be intelligent and given that 'out of habit' also rules out explanations in terms of pleasure, enjoyment, or any kind of intrinsic motivation, it is obvious enough why the intelligent adaptability of a rational code as well as spontaneous delight in practising it and in pursuing worth-while activities are in stark opposition to things that are done 'out of habit'. But, as I have tried to show, they are not so opposed to habits as mere descriptions of types of action. Habits need not be exercised out of force of habit.

The fact, however, that they very often *are* brings me to my empirical point, which is that there are a great number of things which we do in fact do out of habit, and this is essential if our minds are to be set free to attend to other things. . . . It is also the case that in some people whom, in extreme cases, we describe as compulsives, the force of habit is so strong that it militates against intelligent performance and disrupts the rest of man's life. Tidiness and cleanliness are in general sound moral habits because they save time and health and permit efficient and intelligent performance of countless other things. But if a woman is so obsessed with them that she tries to impress the stamp of the operating theatre on the nursery and bedroom of young children, she may well have reached the point where her habits disrupt not only her domestic bliss but also her own capacity for intelligent adaptation and for enjoyment of things that are worth enjoying.

And so we stand at the door of the nursery which is the gateway to moral education. For it is here, in all probability, that the pattern of character-traits and the manner of exercising them is laid down. It is here that habits are first formed in a manner which may lead to the development of compulsives, obsessives, Puritans, and impractical ideologues. To explain how this probably happens would involve a careful examination of cognitive development and the role of extrinsic and intrinsic motivation in childhood. I could not begin to tackle this vast subject in this paper. I have only tried to explain and to resolve the *theoretical* paradox of moral education, not to develop a positive theory of rational child-rearing.

Aristotle put the matter very well when he said: 'But the virtues we get by first exercising them, as also happens in the case of the arts as well. For the things we have to learn before we can do them, we learn by doing them, e.g. men become builders by building and lyre players by playing the lyre; so do we become just by doing just acts, temperate by doing temperate acts, brave by doing brave acts. . . . It makes no small difference then, whether we form habits of one kind or another from our very youth; it makes a great difference or rather all the difference. . . .' [6]

But from the point of view of moral education it makes all the difference, too, at what age and in what manner such habits are formed, especially under what aspect particular acts are taught. For it is only if habits are developed in a certain kind of way that the paradox of moral education can be avoided in practice. This is a matter about which psychologists and practical teachers will have much more to say than philosophers. For I have only tried to resolve the theoretical paradox of moral education in a theoretical manner.

Bacon once said that the discourse of philosophers is like the stars; it sheds little light because it is so high. But when it is brought nearer the earth, as I hope it has been in this paper, it still can only shed light on where empirical research needs to be done and where practical judgments have to be made. It is no substitute for either.

[6] Aristotle, *Nicomachean Ethics*, Bk. II, Chs. 3, 4.

Bibliography

I. OTHER WORKS ON EDUCATION BY OUR AUTHORS BESIDES THOSE QUOTED

Dewey, J. *Experience and Education.* New York: Macmillan, 1938. Available in paperback. [One of Dewey's more recent works.]

Dworkin, M. S. (ed.). *Dewey on Education.* New York: Bureau of Publications, Teachers College, Columbia Univ., 1959. Paperback. [Includes most of Dewey's earlier writings on education.]

Maritain, J. *The Education of Man,* ed. D. and I. Gallagher. Garden City, N.Y.: Doubleday, 1962.

Peters, R. S. "Education as Initiation," *Philosophy of Education—A British View,* R. Archambault (ed.). London: Routledge, 1964.

Whitehead, A. N. *Science and Philosophy.* New York: Philosophical Library, 1948. Paperback. [Part III is on education.]

II. WORKS ON EDUCATION BY OTHER RECENT PHILOSOPHERS:

Ducasse, C. J. "What can Philosophy Contribute to Educational Theory?" *Harvard Educational Review,* **XXVIII** (1958), pp. 285–297. [Useful short statement. Reprinted in J. Park (see under IV below).]

Greene, T. M. *Liberal Education Reconsidered.* Cambridge: Harvard Univ. Press, 1953. [Normative, liberal, Christian, idealist.]

Hardie, C. D. *Truth and Fallacy in Educational Theory.* New York: Bureau of Publications, Teachers College, Columbia Univ., 1962. Paperback. [Analytical. First published in 1942.]

Henry, N. B. (ed.). *Modern Philosophies and Education.* ("The 54th Yearbook of the National Society for the Study of Education.") Chicago: Univ. of Chicago Press, 1955. [Statements by a number of recent philosophers.]

Hook, S. *Education for Modern Man.* New York: Knopf, 1963. [Normative, Deweyan.]

Lenz, J. *Philosophy of Education.* Englewood Cliffs, N.J.: Prentice-Hall, 1964. [Analytical and historical.]

O'Connor, D. J. *An Introduction to the Philosophy of Education.* London: Routledge, 1957. [Analytical.]

Russell, B. *Education and the Good Life.* New York: Boni, 1926. Available in paperback. [Interesting, normative, antipragmatist.]

Scheffler, I. *The Language of Education.* Springfield, Ill.: Thomas, 1960. [Analytical.]

III. HISTORICAL VOLUMES

Brumbaugh, R. S., and N. M. Lawrence. *Philosophers on Education: Six Essays.* Boston: Houghton, 1963. Paperback.

Curtis, S. J., and M. E. Boultwood. *A Short History of Educational Ideas.* London: Univ. Tutorial Press Ltd, 1953.

Frankena, W. K. *Three Historical Philosophies of Education.* Chicago: Scott, Foresman Co., 1965. [Aristotle, Kant, Dewey.]

Price, K. *Education and Philosophical Thought.* Boston: Allyn, 1962. [Selections with introductions.]

IV. VOLUMES ON CONTEMPORARY AUTHORS AND MOVEMENTS

Brameld, T. *Philosophies of Education in Cultural Perspective.* New York: Dryden, 1955. [A "reconstructionist" on progressivism, essentialism, and perennialism.]

Brubacher, J. S. (ed.). *Philosophies of Education.* Chicago: National Society for the Study of Education, 1942. [Various statements of position.]

Hook, S. *John Dewey: An Intellectual Portrait.* New York: Day, 1939.

Kneller, G. F. *Existentialism and Education.* New York: Philosophical Library, 1958.

Park, J. (ed.). *Selected Readings in the Philosophy of Education,* 2d ed. New York: Macmillan, 1963. [Usual approach but up-to-date.]

Scheffler, I., (ed.). *Philosophy and Education.* Boston: Allyn, 1958. [A collection of analytical essays.]